The Journey From the Head to the Heart and Beyond ---

Fr. Stephen Valenta, OFM Conv.

NIHIL OBSTAT:
　　Giles Van Wormer, OFM Conv.
　　Minister Provincial

IMPRIMATUR:
　　+The Most Reverend Howard J. Hubbard, D.D.
　　Bishop of Albany, New York
　　January 23, 1997

Library of Congress Catalog Card No.: In Process

ISBN: 1-890390-00-3

Book Design and Typesetting: Archangel Crusade of Love™
　　　　　　　　　　　　　　　　24490 Broadway Ave.
　　　　　　　　　　　　　　　　Cleveland, Ohio 44146
　　　　　　　　　　　　　　　　216 439-3034

Printed in U.S.A.

May God give a special blessing to all of the good people who have helped me put this book together. Without them, it would have never come to be. Mother Mary knows who they are. From Her I ask for them a special motherly embrace.

TABLE OF CONTENTS

FOREWORD

One day while Father Valenta was staying with us at Our Lady of the Holy Spirit Center in Cincinnati, I went to him and asked him to please explain to me what Our Lady meant in Medjugorje when she asked us to pray with the heart! I know how to pray, or at least I thought I did, but I never reflected on Our Lady's asking us to pray with the heart. That must be something different from regular prayer and something definitely more intense, I thought. Father was very ready to explain to me what Our Lady meant, and it has helped me intensely to attempt to pray better not only with the mind but especially with the heart. I won't go into the process that Father explained to me because he says it much better than I can in his book. I ask the reader to read and re-read this dynamic book to help each and every one of you with your spiritual growth in your prayer life. Father gives us such a beautiful insight into ourselves and especially our relationship with God the Father, Son and Holy Spirit, as well as with Our Blessed Lady. Once you begin to read this book you will want to continue to the end very quickly. But wait! Father tells you to take your time, re-read and meditate and contemplate... such good advice. The spiritual life is always a process of new beginnings and it takes a lot of practice to almost begin anew each day. But coming into direct contact with a loving God is worth all the effort we can muster.

I urge you to read (with the mind and heart) all that Father presents to you on the written pages of this book. Come to grips with some of the problems that Father presents to you and then begin to put your complete trust in His love, His mercy and His forgiveness.

Father Valenta gives us a beautiful summary and work-book of what the spiritual life is all about. I thank him for this wonderful work of love, helping to bring us all to a much closer understanding of God's great love for us who are true creatures of God, body and soul. My deepest gratitude to Father Valenta who asked me to write the foreword to this most important work, a work that is most necessary , in my humble opinion, for every Christian and Catholic in today's society.

Father R. Leroy Smith
President of Our Lady of the Holy Spirit Center
Norwood, Ohio

PREFACE

"I tell you, he will see to it that justice is done for them speedily. But when the Son of Man comes, will He find faith on earth?"

(Luke 18:8)

W hat I am about to write should have been written thirty years ago. The fact that it was not has made life more difficult for many. Who is to say that perhaps even souls which have passed on could have been saved? On the other hand, Divine Providence has everything and everyone within Its loving concern. If it should have been written, then, by God's calculations, it would have been written. God, as our loving Father, uses anything and everything to win people to Himself, anything short of outright force. He does everything in the most perfect way. If I sit here writing at this point in time, according to His plan, it is the best possible time.

The reason that I feel that what is written here should have been written long ago is that the contents are of the utmost importance. At this moment I have somewhat of an idea what I will write because I have heard it said already many times. For several years I have been traveling from sea to shining sea and beyond, giving workshops on, "How To Pray with the Heart." The fruits of these workshops have been so astounding, so rewarding, so lasting, deeply touching the hearts and minds of the participants. Lives have changed for the better, souls have been unsnarled, hundreds upon hundreds have been liberated, for what has been said was the truth, and it has set many free. God alone knows the full extent of the good that was done through these workshops, but by way of contact through the mails and by way of the phone, I know that the Holy Spirit has made use of the workshops to do for men and women what He could not have done otherwise. What had been imparted in the conferences within the course of two days is what will be, by and large, presented through the following pages. The truths shared then in speaking will be the same truths, but now given in writing.

At the very beginning of the first conference of each workshop, I would relate to the assembled that I presented myself before them with an empty head. I personally had nothing planned to say, no script, no memorization. I let the people present know that I had placed myself completely under the influence of the Holy Spirit. Why? Because I did not know the people and I did not know precisely what each and every person there needed to hear. "The Spirit knows each one of you intimately," I said, and "He knows full well what each of you need to hear for your betterment of life, for a healing, for the attaining of a closer relationship with God, our Father, Jesus, our Brother, and the Holy Spirit, the Giver of Life. I am emptied out so that He can speak to you through me in whatever way, by my own life's experiences, failures and gains, even gestures and examples, so that what He has been trying to get through to you and could not, for one reason or another, He will be able to do now. This workshop is custom-made. It is fitted just for you who are here. So that each one of you in a greater or smaller way may gain something for the taking of your time, and making the effort to have taken the time to be here."

I want you, dear reader, to know that I will do the very same thing now and I will take on the very same posture by putting myself under the influence of the Spirit for the very same reason as in the workshops, that He may do for you through your reading what He had done for so many through me in speaking.

You may be wondering how it could be that anyone would be so bold as to say, "I place myself under the influence of the Holy Spirit." Your wonderment is valid and to help you along, I will share with you a bit of my past. I had lived in a hermitage for some eighteen years. While there, among many other things, I conducted a weekly mini-retreat every Sunday. As the people were assembled in the chapel, I would prepare myself in the sacristy by putting out of my head all of my own thoughts. I would not leave the sacristy until and unless I did not have a single thought in my head. The only experience that I housed within me was in my heart, and that was a deep trust that, given the opportunity, the Spirit living within me would do better for the people than I myself could. With a phrase, He could clear up something for someone present that would ordinarily take from two to three paragraphs. To leave the material for each conference to Him was something I had gradually learned to do. At the time when I was to give my first conference for the very first mini-retreat, I said to Him in prayer, "Holy Spirit, if You are really living within me, as I believe that You have been since my Baptism, I will risk it. I will get rid of my own thoughts in order that You might present Yours." I trusted Him and He proved Himself to be trustworthy. It has been that way for every conference I have given since. He knows what the people need to hear, so I get out of His way and give Him full reign. So you see, it's not being bold, it is a posture for preaching which has proved itself. It is time tested, and has produced much fruit.

The very same will be the fact for this writing. He knows ahead of time who will be reading this book. I will allow Him free access to my mind and heart that the greatest good can be accomplished for you, the reader, and for others whom He will prompt to pick up this material to read. You may say that I place a great burden on myself not to engage in my own thinking. At the very beginning this was so, but now, after many years, it is the way I live, the way I preach, the way that I now write. When we first were learning how to drive a car, it was not easy. Now, after much practice and driving, it has become second nature. Do believe me, therefore, when I say to you that what you are reading is just for you. I will be writing, not with thought, but with trust. You may have to take my word for it for now, but wait and you will see that what I am saying will prove to be true. This is not being presumptuous. I say what I say from conviction. I know that, as you continue reading, you will be within the loving care of the Holy Spirit. If you are of good will, and I believe that you are, the Holy Spirit will take the initiative to see to it that you will receive graces and be enriched in your spiritual life through your reading.

There is something else that I would like to bring to your attention before beginning. There will be something quite unique in the presentation of what is being written. Whatever is written will have YOU at HEART. Hopefully you will find your reading a pleasant experience because, as the Holy Spirit prompts me what to write, it will not be a generalization, it will be personal, just for you. It is as I will visualize you before me as a specific and special person known to and loved by all of heaven. The entire book will be as a dialogue between you and the Spirit abiding within me. If you plan to read with mere curiosity, you might as well close the book right now and put it away. It won't do you much good. If you intend to read it with your belief motor running and with a desire to become more good than more smart, then continue to read, because what you will read will stick to your spiritual ribs and do much to enhance goodness within you. For best results, pick up the book ONLY when you are prompted to do so by the Holy Spirit. What I am really asking you to do is to read with your heart and not with your head. If the words on the page hit your eyes and then are directed right to the heart, you may read slowly and less, but you will gain more and it will become a part of you right away. If there is something in your reading that will strike you or draw a reaction out of you, put the book down, get into the heart, as in prayer, and let the Spirit resolve it for you. Then pick up the book again to continue to read.

Do not rush through your reading. Take your time. Read only when you are at peace and your heart is in a receptive mode. You may not be able to do all of this right away. Be patient with yourself, tread very lightly and let the Spirit do the greater part. Rely heavily on His Wisdom and His Love for you. As much as possible, enter into your reading prayerfully. Find a quiet place away from noise and distractions. Out of love and concern for yourself, which is proper self-love and not selfishness, give yourself a treat and take time for some spiritual growth.

Allow me to share just one more thing with you. I have not written much in the past. For me it has always been a chore that demanded more discipline than I cared to muster. Most of my priestly ministry has been spent in preaching. I have spent thousands of hours speaking to individuals, to groups large and small. I have also spent many hours before television and taping cameras. One day in prayer it occurred to me that many people learn better by way of the written word than by way of the spoken word. Some draw much of their knowledge through their ears; others through their eyes. It was this realization that finally brought me to tackle what I still believe, at this moment, is something far beyond my capability and endurance, save for God's help. I know that He and Our Lady want it.

Enough said. With all that has been said, we are now both buckled within the loving embrace of the Holy Spirit. Steady as she goes, we are ready for the takeoff!

In order to help the reader to pinpoint any material within this text we have facilitated doing this by breaking each page into 5 line segments.

CHAPTER 1

Urgency of the Moment

> *"O Jerusalem, Jerusalem, you who kill the prophets and stone those sent to you, how many times I yearned to gather your children together, as a hen gathers her young under her wings, but you were unwilling."*
> *(Matt. 23:37)*

Jesus chided the apostles and others because they did not recognize the signs of the times. He referred to the fact that for centuries the prophets spoke of His coming. Scripture was filled with statements about where He would be born, the gentle person He would be, that He would be curing the sick and the maimed. He stood there before them with astonishment that, after all He had done in their presence, they were still blinded to His real identity.

Almost two thousand years later, the very same thing is happening. There are signs beyond an accurate count that mankind is in its end times, having been foretold by Jesus, Himself, as reported in the twenty-fourth chapter of the Gospel of St. Matthew. Especially revealing are the statements in the thirty-seventh, thirty-eighth, and the thirty-ninth verses wherein is written: "For as it was in the days of Noah, so it will be at the coming of the Son of Man. In days before the flood, they were eating and drinking, marrying and giving in marriage, up to the day that Noah entered the ark. They did not know until the flood came and carried them all away. So will it be at the coming of the Son of Man." We are being told that the days of the Second Advent, the days of Jesus' return in glory, are close at hand, even at the door. As prophesied, almost everyone is so occupied with the things of the world, the things of the flesh, the things that fill every moment, that, when those things that are being foretold begin to happen, they will take most of the world by surprise unto devastation, as they did the people of Noah's time.

Reports of uncommon happenings are coming through the media continuously. The news of unusual weather keeps streaming in, reports of one calamity after another. These include earthquakes, tornadoes, hurricanes, drought, blizzards, and floods. We learn of wars, ethnic cleansing, humans being massacred by the hundreds of thousands, mysterious epidemics taking thousands upon thousands from the land of the living, terrorists, with their explosives devastating millions upon millions with crippling fear. On the other hand, there are

the apparitions of the Blessed Virgin Mary. Though she warns
of a purification, persecution, chastisement, she comes forth
with the hopeful words that the world is heading for a new era,
an era of peace and harmony, a time within which Jesus will
establish His kingdom on earth. She announces that Satan will
be chained in hell and evil will disappear from the face of
the earth.

You and I are living in the midst of it all. So much is
happening all around us so rapidly and with such an impact on
our daily lives that we scarcely know what to do, where to
hide, how to prepare. It seems that we are no longer our own,
that huge forces closing in from all around us are ready to snuff
out every hope, every bit of cherished peace, every smallest
bit of joy. The worst of it is that all of these happenings and
conditions keep us wrapped up and even imprisoned in our
minds. Our days and much of our nights are spent in
wondering what might be next, spinning our wheels by trying
to figure out solutions for ourselves. What all of this does to
each of us is to smother any activity of the heart in which
abides faith, hope, love, obedience and many other fulfilling
and liberating qualities. We are forced into a fragmentation of
our individual human system. We know so much and can do
so little. We find ourselves powerless to override living in
a heaviness of soul under the darkness of an enervating
helplessness.

An urgency does exist. No matter how much thinking goes
on in this generation in which you and I are living, no one is
coming up with answers that can even remotely ease the
conditions we are in. Even with all the thinking being done by
millions and millions of people who have come to the realization that some solution must be found to resolve the conditions, nothing positive is forthcoming. To the contrary, despite
the effort that is being made to find human solutions to a
weary and war-torn world, things are going from bad to worse.
Evil abounds. The commandments of God are ignored. The
world says, "Think, think, think." God, our Creator, knows

what needs to be done, and what He is saying is, "Obey, obey, obey."

God has dealt with generations like ours before. In the time of Jeremiah, the prophet, the people had turned completely away from God. We are able to capture God's attitude toward His people in what He instructed Jeremiah to do. He was to obtain a loincloth, wear it for a time, and then stash it in a cleft of rock. Later the Lord God sent him to fetch it and, lo and behold, it was nothing but rot, absolutely useless but to be thrown out. God chose to make a point to His people. Here is what He said in Jeremiah's own words: "In the same way I will rot the pride of Judah and the great pride of Jerusalem. These wicked people, who refuse to listen to My words, who follow the stubbornness of their hearts and go after other gods to serve and worship them, will be like this loincloth — completely useless! For as a loincloth is bound around a man's loins, so I bound the whole house of Israel and the whole house of Judah to Me," declares the LORD, " to be My people for My renown and praise and honor. But they have not listened." (Jer. 13: 9-11) Punishment did follow out of justice, as also out of mercy, to humble His people.

In this moment of urgency, there is but one solution that is available, that is valid, and that is extremely hopeful. It is for our generation to make the journey from the head to the heart. This generation is made up of individual persons. It does you and me no good to moan and groan about conditions. Nothing will improve unless and until you and I, living units of this generation, decide to do it right, that is, that you and I arrange for ourselves to make this journey in order to find within our hearts wisdom and strength to wade through it all, and come forth with sanity, hopefulness and joy. These are positive elements that we could introduce into our life, into our everyday actions. The distance between the physical head and the physical heart is very short. Only inches separate them. The journey, as it really is, can take months, years, and even a lifetime. The journey is not easy to make. It has its

pitfalls, it has its ups and downs, dark and light hours and sometimes days. It is a journey that Jesus invites you to make. For myself, I have already made the journey and am prepared to give you encouragement to join me at the journey's end and
5 beyond. I assure you it is worth all the blood and sweat that it takes to get there.

By Jesus' own admission, His kingdom is found "within," carrying a cross, going through the narrow gate, abandoning mother, father, and all others, suffering violence, becoming as
10 little children, remaining within the sheepfold under the leadership and guidance of the Shepherd. It is when we enter into belief, trust, love, and obedience that we can move forward through it all and come out purified, selfless, Christ-centered, Jesus-like. Finding our way out of the head and into the heart
15 makes it possible to do just what it is that we are given life for, namely, to love God with our whole heart, strength, soul, mind, and to love our neighbor as we love ourselves. Living within the heart is the only safe road to arrive at the very purpose of our existence which is to know, love, and serve God, nothing
20 more, nothing less.

It may all seem so rigid, so rigorous, so hopeless. Who in their right mind can even dare to stop thought long enough to love and to live giving loving service? Knowledge seems to offer the only way out of the maze in which we find ourselves.
25 Who would dare to give up searching with the mind for answers for one second, lest hopelessness set in for fear of not finding any and having to live imprisoned by external forces? We are trained from our earliest days that if we don't do our lessons, we will not pass into the next grade. In our adult years,
30 we come to believe that it is what you know, who you know, that will bring success. To make a journey from knowing where we are, to a place in which we might feel uncomfortable is frightening to say the least. Why abandon that in which we experience security for that which is nebulous, so out of
35 reach, so undefined?

Checking once again the Table of Contents can bring on a sense of futility, but it can also bring on an experience of encouragement. To make the journey from the head to the heart will invite challenges, but the path has been traveled by many, all of whom have found unending peace and joy. If you would consider the book that you are holding as a traveler's guide, as a handbook to be referred to day in and day out, even somewhat as an owner's manual, step-by-step, chapter by chapter, inch by inch, it will prove to be a cinch. As in every journey, there will be times to rest, to refresh, to obtain some nourishment, stopping for a bit and once again moving on. The urgency of the moment can haunt us as a spectrum of gloom and doom. It need not. The journey, though uphill, amidst thorns and seemingly unsurmountable ledges and dangerous cliffs and crevices, comes with a built-in Guide, the Holy Spirit. He knows the way well. He will assure you often by inner consolations, by on-the-spot "spiritual shots in the arm," making it clear that it will be well worth your while to continue. Progressing gradually, and with courage, you will assuredly reach the summit. Summit? Yes, you will find it within the depth of your heart.

CHAPTER 2

At the Starting Line

> *"He saved us and called us to a holy life, not according to our works but according to His own design and the grace bestowed on us in Christ Jesus before time began, ..."*
>
> *(2 Tim. 1:9)*

A n athlete about to compete in a running race crouches low at the starting line to have the best advantage for the forward thrust the second the gun goes off. What the athlete's thoughts and feelings are at that point has much to do with whether he or she wins the race. If thoughts of confidence are being entertained, the feelings that go along with these thoughts become a source of energy to the muscles of the legs. If, on the other hand, there are thoughts of discouragement, say because of the knowledge that one of the other runners has won more races, these thoughts generate feelings that indeed hamper the agility of the same muscles. It will be the same with you as you take on this journey. If within you there is at least a degree of confidence that you already have sufficient willpower to see the journey through to its finish, grace from the Holy Spirit will be able to accomplish much for you. If, on the other hand, you are entertaining doubts as to whether you can indeed enter into a heart life, your doubt would be a factor of resistance to the power and generosity of the Holy Spirit. Whatever may be the case, I would ask you to put your inner feelings on hold until you allow yourself to give thought to matters that might prove to be beneficial.

Your life, in all of its details, is known in its completeness only to God. As God, your Creator and Father, He looks favorably upon you especially as He watches over you in this effort that you are making to draw closer to Him through the journey into which you are already putting forth effort. Even the courage which you had to pick up this book, to open it, and to get this far in your reading, has already come from the generosity of His Spirit. He knew you even as you were within your mother's womb. It was He Who arranged that you be there. Whether you realize it or not, He has played a great part in your life, such a part that is mind-boggling, a part which He will let you in on once you enter into eternity. For reasons known only to Himself, He wanted you to live within this specific generation, at this specific time in history. For you to gain a few insights into your life that will undoubtedly assist you at the onset of your journey, I would ask you to direct your mind's eye to the following scenario.

You have been placed in the twentieth century by God for a definite purpose, to accomplish something very special. He has also determined that you be on earth during the closing years of this century. This is by His Own design, with specifics within His Mind, as to why He has chosen you to be a part of this particular generation. Those who are trained to evaluate centuries and generations would be quick to point out to you that this is either the best or the worst generation of the best or worst century. Some might boastfully point to the tremendous technological developments, the superb contributions to mankind of the space discoveries, the improvements in how people travel from place to place, the convenience stores and the fast food eateries. Others would say that despite all of these niceties, this is the worst century of all and that the present generation cannot be compared with any other for the evil that goes on therein. Within the span of this century there have been two world wars, numerous devastating civil wars, genocides, and mass murders. In this generation, the disturbances of nature by way of hurricanes, earthquakes, droughts, tornadoes, floods, blizzards, and volcano eruptions, have broken records. The terrorism of this generation has no equal. Billions are being held hostage and victimized. Never, never in all of history have so many tiny lives been snuffed out while still in the wombs of their mothers with the help of modern technology.

Bringing the scenario closer to home, some learned evaluators would look upon the happenings in the Catholic Church and point out that this century produced some of the greatest Popes and one of the most fruitful Ecumenical Councils in all of Church history. Others, on the contrary, would point at the incomprehensible confusion among the faithful, the virtual disappearance of reverence, the unprecedented exodus of priests and religious, the tampering with Sacred Scriptures, and the manipulation of doctrine by the theologians.

This is the generation and the century into which your loving Father put you. Why you? Why in the midst of all this? He knows why. It is fundamental that what God did in bringing you into life within this point in time He did with wisdom, love, and purpose.

Ponder the obstacles to the enjoyment of a full life that you have had to surmount just to survive. If the heart-life was established by God as the best possible life and if He truly wanted you to have the best, why did He put you into the midst of a generation that is so mentally orientated, into a generation imprisoned in the mind, into a generation that idolizes knowledge, trivia, and sports scores? Do not be disappointed if you don't know the answer. There are a couple of other "whys" you might want to consider. From your earliest days, even before you were sent off to kindergarten, and before you knew the difference between right and wrong you had already been formed by what you saw on TV. The entire formative culture sent you off to school to learn so that you could become smart, smart so that you could get a good job, a good job so that you could make lots of money, lots of money so that you could buy anything and everything you want. Why were you thrown the curve ball of society impressing the message upon you that, for you to succeed in life, you must think, think, think, study, study, study, learn, learn, learn? Perhaps now you can better understand why a journey from the head to the heart needs to be made. In this generation, the emphasis in formation is not on goodness, as God intends, but on smarts. Jesus, when on earth, did not give the directive, "Thou shalt be smart!" He did say, "Thou shalt be good!" As you have probably already discerned, smarts is a quality of the mind; goodness is a quality of the heart.

So you see, you were put into life with a handicap by way of what you met up with once you were in it. It would occur to me by the fact that you have this book in hand, that even though society has done a number on you, you are nonetheless keeping your head above water. There are those (and many they are) who, once they came into life, met up with such obstacles in their formation that they turned out to be cripples, not having the foggiest notion of what life is all about nor any idea of why they are on earth. All of this raises questions in your mind. I know. I myself had to address the same questions. The answer that you can give yourself is to go back to what you had, no doubt, been already taught somewhere along the line; namely, God is Good, He is Love, He is All Powerful. Every single thing He does or allows to happen comes out of wisdom and His deep concern for each and every person whom He has chosen to place upon this earth. There are no exceptions.

There is something else that would throw some additional light on your thinking and would possibly offer some courage to your aspirations to enjoy a more fulfilling and joyful life. It is the need for you to take responsibility in dealing with the evil that surrounds you, the evil into which you have been placed by your God. This evil is not primarily the same as was mentioned earlier, that is, putting smarts above the quality of goodness. Rather, it is an evil that comes from the hardness of hearts. What makes the difference between a hard and cold heart and a soft and warm heart? And why do some have one instead of the other? The fact that hardness of heart is a pronounced characteristic of this generation is a matter of fact. God has given you life and has decreed that you be a part of this generation. Why? Don't let it trouble you that you don't have an answer. Someday you will. Do know, however, that your living in the midst of all this is by design. God put you on earth to accomplish something that only you can. You might reflect for a moment or two as to what this purpose might be.

CHAPTER 3

You as You, as Is

"Then the Lord God formed the man from the dust of the ground and breathed into his nostrils the breath of life, and man became a living being."

(Gen. 2:7)

"As is" is a descriptive phrase that is used in the advertising of merchandise, such as automobiles, large appliances, and electronic devices. It gives the message to the prospective buyer that the commodity up for sale is to be bought with no after-sale responsibilities to the seller. What you see is what you get. Take it or leave it. It is being used here, dear reader, to help you better understand just what it is that you are when you say of yourself, "I am a human being. That is what I am, no more, no less. I have come into life 'as is.'"

What is it that you are when you say you are a human being? It is you as a person who has entered into life with a body and a soul. The instant that the egg was fertilized by the sperm, God took direct action to create your soul. Within the soul is housed the person. When your parents begot you, it was not within their power to create your soul. Your soul is spiritual and, as such, it could have been brought into existence only by God Who alone could create a spiritual being. Your parents made it possible for God to engage His creative power to bring your soul into existence. Each of your parents contributed respectively an essential element, the sperm and the egg. When the sperm and the egg came together, fertilization took place. It was at that precise moment that God created your soul. This is what is called the moment of conception. It was then that you became a full-fledged human being. God and your parents worked together as a team. You could not have come into life with just a body. Nor could you have come into life just as a soul. The body had to be with your soul and your soul had to be within your body in order for you to have been able to come into the world as a human being.

Your body and soul have their own distinctive characteristics. They are fused together as one unique and independent unit. Though your soul can exist without your body, your body cannot exist without your soul. Once God calls the soul to Himself in death, the body becomes lifeless. During the span of your life on earth they work together, each offering specific qualities to allow you a full earthly life.

God has given your body five senses: sight, hearing, taste, smell, and touch. With these you are enjoying varied experiences, each completely different from the other. It is absolutely awesome how God has put these together so that each adds a bit more to the enjoyment of your life. How intricately is each one of the senses designed! It is truly a remarkable feat for Him to put such refinement into each sense. What would life be for you without any one of them? It might be an opportune time to take ten seconds to whisper a "thank you" to Him for them. They are His gifts to you.

Your soul too has its own special capabilities called faculties. Your soul has a mind which I have spoken of as the head because it works through the brain, and your soul has a will, which I have referred to as the heart because it works through the physical heart. It is with your mind that you reach out to truth. It is with your will that you reach out to goodness. With your mind you can think, remember, speculate, imagine, seek truth, search for solutions, evaluate, analyze, and more. It is a marvelous invention, a tremendous gift. It is also capable of entering into a receptive mode in which it could listen to what others are saying to you as well as to what God might want to say to you.

The will is very special. With it you can believe, trust, love, obey, forgive, be grateful, be reverent, worship, cope, carry out disciplines, and more. Its greatest asset is that it is the seat of freedom. God gave you your will so that you could make choices and so that you could choose to love Him as well as other human beings. Your will, because of its quality of freedom, resists all force. God could have forced you to be good. He chose not to. He wants that you make the choice to be good. Of all the gifts that He has bestowed upon you, this is one is truly unique. I will share with you more about the mind and will, that is the head and the heart, in greater depth a bit later. For now, let this suffice.

At this point in your journey, I need your undivided attention. When speaking of yourself as a person, you say "I AM a person." When speaking of your body you say "I HAVE a body." When speaking of your soul, you say "I HAVE a soul." You do not say "I am a body, I am a soul." When you speak of your will, you say "I have a will." When speaking of your mind, you say "I have a mind." You will notice that it is only when making reference to your person that you can say "I AM." All else is something that you as a person have in your possession, for your use. This must be interesting because it reminds you that here is where your real importance rests, in your person. Only your person is a WHO. All the other parts of you, be it your mind, your will, your eyes, and everything else, are WHATS. All of your WHATS are at the disposal of your WHO. You as a person are to take responsibility for your life.

God has given you another gift. It is the ability to express yourself emotionally. Emotions belong neither to the body nor to the soul, but can be expressed through each of them. Some common expressions are: sadness, elation, impatience, anger, frustration, and loneliness. These and others are commonly spoken of as "feelings." Somewhere within you are also what are known as passions. These, too, are neither of the body nor of the soul but work through them. They can be best identified within you as "cravings." Your passions and emotions are in need of your person so that with the use of your mind and will you can guide and govern them. Left to themselves, they can get out of hand. Just as a captain is in charge of a ship, just as you are in charge of your car, so you as a person are in charge of your body, your soul, your emotions, and your passions. Each and every one of your personal "whats," are to be guided by you to your ultimate goal. I have already mentioned this goal to you. You have been put on earth only for a time. You are being given an opportunity by God freely to acknowledge Him for who He is and to recognize who you are in relation to who He is. You have a sublime destiny. This destiny is to enter into and enjoy a love relationship with God while on earth so that at the end of your life, by giving Him loving service, you can be rewarded for your goodness. Your ultimate goal is to enjoy an eternity of happiness with God in heaven.

Now for a little surprise! There is something more that has been given to you by God. It is an extremely special gift. It is Baptism. It is easy for you to say somewhat nonchalantly, "Oh yes, I was baptized." It's much, much more than that. Through Baptism you have been given a new birth. You have been born again. You have been born twice, once into what is called the natural life, and the other, which is known as the supernatural life. These are not mere terms. Something very exciting took place when they brought you into the church and had you baptized. What was so special about it is that through Baptism you were raised to a new plateau of life, one that makes it possible for you, while still on this earth, to share in GOD'S life. This is something that you cannot simply take for granted. The fact that you have been baptized will make a vast difference in your life here on earth and, for certain, in your life beyond death.

By sharing in God's life, you have at your disposal knowledge and power that you would not have otherwise. This knowledge and power that flows from God into your soul will make life tremendously delightful. For you to govern your body, your mind, your will, your emotions, and passions is no easy task. Put together, they are like a wild horse that needs to be tamed. This special knowledge is yours to make use of during your entire life. It will offer you a better appreciation of life in general and many parts of it in particular. It will make clear to you what to do in life so that you can guide your "ship" to port, that is, that you can finally attain your ultimate goal — eternal happiness in heaven with God.

The special powers given to you at Baptism flow through your will. You are given energy that is superhuman. With this superhuman power you have the ability to overcome great hardships. You have the power with you will to discipline your mind and to keep it focused on deeper truths of life. With your divinely empowered will, you can keep your emotions and passions in check so that they are not an extra burden but rather are trained to give you added agility as you go through life. The qualities that you have received through Baptism will be discussed at length in succeeding chapters.

5   You can readily see that "as is" you are a bundle of values a bundle that cannot be bought with all the money in the world. God gave you to you as a gift and made that gift more perfect for you to share in His life through Baptism. That means that you are very special to Him, more special than all of the other created things in the world put together. It also means that it is advisable that you give recognition to this specialness, appreciate it, live with it, and make the best use of it.

CHAPTER 4

Your Dignity as a Person

"So God created man in His own image, in the image of God He created him; male and female He created them."

(Gen. 1:27)

*M*ay I have the pleasure of reminding you that living your life in the world today, during the last half of this twentieth century is like swimming upstream in a fast flowing river. For you to dare to do something like that, you had better be a good swimmer. A life like yours could be easily lost in attempting a feat of that sort. A similar experience would have you in a sailboat tacking against the wind when an unexpected gust of wind, more powerful than usual, hits your sail and flips your boat. You end up in the water with land a half mile away.

As you live your life today, you encounter enormous opposition if, with a value system that you have received through your Faith, you make an effort to forge ahead against many other value systems most of which are in direct opposition to what you hold. The culture in which you live is a mental culture. Thinking is what most people do most of the time, for long hours of the day and perhaps through many hours of the night. The force of thought is like that of a raging river. With the media, the computerized expressway, the TV blasting away hour after hour, junk mail that make its way into homes, the political, economic, and other promotional materials forcing their way into every city and every town, the world propaganda of this generation is enough to drive anyone to the depths of frustration. The values of the secular humanistic world, the values of a world immersed in a materialistic, atheistic, hedonistic, pragmatic, and utilitarian environment, come at you continuously knocking at your mind's door soliciting your acceptance. Could it be possible for anyone like yourself with your values to stand up against a barrage such as this? Let me assure you that it is possible. As you continue your journey you will learn not only how to maintain yourself in your value system but also how to thrive in the face of its opposition.

The most powerful weapon being used against you is the attack on your human dignity. It comes by way of glorifying the body, denying the existence of the soul, and attacking the very nature of personhood. You are recognized best by your number and soon by your fingerprints, and in time by an implanted chip. Your greatest value by way of modern appraisal lies in your productivity, in your spending power, and in your obeying the law. You are treated today by most as a THING rather than as a PERSON. You are commonly appreciated for WHAT you can do and/or WHAT you have instead of WHO you are.

When God created you, He created you as a PERSON. That means that you were created in His image and likeness. that you have Godlike qualities. These qualities distinguish you from all the "whats" in the world. To God you are of more value than all the 'whats' in the entire universe. In order for you to appreciate better your God-given value you might want to spend a little time munching on this wholesome truth: God the Father is a PERSON. God the Son is a PERSON. God the Holy Spirit is a PERSON. YOU are a PERSON. You may slam your fist on the table, you may pound the floor with your foot, and shout at the top of your voice: "I am a PERSON! ! !"

The first one you must convince of this truth is yourself. If you are like anyone else, the ordinary treatment that you get maybe even from some of your own family helps you to forget WHO you are. You would do yourself a great favor if you would insist on accepting yourself as a person made in the image and likeness of God. For your own well-being, there is an urgent need for you to know and value your own true worth. If YOU don't, no one else will!

There is a recommendation that I would like to make to you. It is this: As you get out of bed and slip into the bathroom, look at yourself in the mirror, bow to yourself and say, "Good morning, Your Highness." Take it for what is it worth, but mean it! You do have worth! You have dignity! Learn to treat yourself with respect. Your mind may nag at you because of your faults and limitations. So be it! Keep reminding it of who you are and give it a command once in awhile to get off your back. There is a fine line here. You may not always be happy about the things you do, but you ought never to give up your happiness over who you are. If you would but recall often that God Himself looks up to you and that each Person of the Blessed Trinity has a special interest in you, your spirit would find peace. The challenge in everyday living is for you to maintain within yourself recognition of your importance. It is not that you take this importance to yourself. It is given to you by your God.

What is being said here does not fall into the category of SELFISHNESS. It falls into the category of SELF-LOVE. There is a world of difference between the two. Selfishness is expressed when you grab for yourself what YOU want even at the expense of doing harm to others. Self-Love is giving to yourself that which is best for you and which you deserve to have because of who you are. The Lord said, "Love your neighbor as you love yourself." Make note of that! How can you love your neighbor if you do not love yourself? As I travel the country and beyond, it is not cancer or AIDS that is the worst thing I find. What I find to be the worst is SELF-HATRED. People instinctively know that they are not on target, that they are not living as their internal sense tells them, consequently, as they hate what they do, without always realizing it, they also hate who they are. Know this: if you hate yourself, you will also hate your neighbor. This massive hatred of self is reflected in our headlines. On the other hand, if you love and respect your-self, you will love and respect everyone else, not giving consid-eration to their WHATS. Even when Jesus directs us to love our enemies, He requires us to love them for WHO they are, even if we don't agree with WHAT they do.

Mark my word! Your life will change as you begin to express gratitude to God for creating you and giving you instant worth. This is not pride. This is the truth! You DO have worth. It is God given!

There is still another bit of truth that will bring joy to your heart. No one in the whole world is just like YOU. You are absolutely UNIQUE. This is not just saying so. It IS the truth. God's creative power makes it so. God does not make use of mass production. He creates every single person individually. Believe it or not, you are CUSTOM-made! What is even more exciting is that, from the time of Adam and Eve, there has NEVER been anyone just like YOU. What is even more awesome is that, as long as the world lasts, God will NEVER create anyone just like YOU. It is absolutely fascinating! One side effect of this is that you never have to compete with others. You can free yourself of tons of anguish. You never have to put others down so that you can put yourself up in their estimation. You can always stand on your own feet with your head raised high.

When I was a youngster, I worked in my Dad's store. One day he was cutting up a chicken because some lady wanted it for Sunday dinner. After he had taken out the insides, I looked in, as a little kid would likely do, and exclaimed, "Dad, why did you kill this chicken? Look at the eggs we could have sold." Inside there was a progression of the yoke from the tiniest to a yoke that was to have hatched in a day or two. In addition, there were some fifty little white "dots" that would have become eggs. The point is, within you, God has put numberless little "dots" that are potential talents. The development of these talents would make you a TALENTED PERSON. Never should you have to look to the left or right to see what other people have or what they can do. There is plenty within you for future development to keep you busy for the rest of your life.

Can you imagine what a change for the better will take place in your life once you learn to give yourself reverence for whom God made you to be and to become? You will also be in awe of every other human being. You will find it easy to look UP to individuals, and spare yourself the sadness that enters when you look DOWN on them.

Let me say again for the sake of emphasis: It all begins with self-respect and an admiration of God for making you who you really are. Once you achieve this, even your WHATS will improve. Result? You experience joy. When you do, you will add a ray of hope to this vale of tears.

It should be clear to you by now how in what has been stated above — allowing the marvelous truths about you to seep into the mind — that the next action for the heart to take is to accept the true value of yourself which the mind presents to it, and savor it as something very real. You will learn more about this later in your journey.

For now, I have a favor to ask of you. I trust you will grant it. Here it is: Would you kindly stop reading for about ten minutes and enter into yourself with a prayerful stance and ask the Holy Spirit to help you improve your estimation of yourself? Bring before your mind's eye who you really are, a creature made in the image and likeness of your God. You, as a person, have a resemblance to Him though it be on a different level. God IS love, you HAVE love. God IS truth, you HAVE truth. God IS good, you HAVE goodness. God IS power, you HAVE power. Get it? Now, don't forget the favor.

CHAPTER 5

Inner Conflicts

"Even so, on the outside you appear righteous, but inside you are filled with hypocrisy and evildoing."
(Matt. 23:28)

"Watch and pray that you may not undergo the test The spirit is willing, but the flesh is weak."
(Mark 14:38)

Y ou will remember that I had mentioned that this journey from the head to the heart will not be an easy one to make. I remind you of this because I am fully aware of an assortment of conflicts that can stage themselves within your soul. In spiritual directions and counseling sessions, I have encountered within souls anywhere from a small and insignificant civil war up to a potential World War III. Among the emotions there can be cross conflicts between one emotion and another, one combination of emotions against another combination. Passions, too, can become quite unruly. The mind can be confused beyond immediate help. The will might be anywhere from being slovenly to being completely in charge of the whole spiritual and psychological network. The combination of inner conflicts could be very many, wherein lies the condition of anxiety and restlessness, or it could be that there are none. This latter condition is that which brings peace of soul. If at present your own soul may be experiencing some minor or major turbulence, be at peace. It is par for the course. There is no conflict that cannot be straightened out by your trust in God's grace.

Your interior system, which includes the whole of your spiritual qualities, could be in utter disorder. If order is to be attained, a search needs to be made in order to find a starting point. In most instances, it is within the will. Whether it lacks power or has so much power that it bulldozes itself into the rest of the spiritual or emotional centers, it cannot even begin to start a process of bringing things into order without training. When there is a lack of power coming forth from the will, the mind is especially effected. When there is no disciplined power of will available, the mind is dominated extensively by the emotions or the passions or even by what comes in through the bodily senses. If the mind is not capable of discernment, it cannot possibly direct any action that might bring the soul to peace. One of the greatest sources of conflict is that which pits the body against the soul. If I were to say that ninety out of a hundred situations of conflict would be caused by the body, that would be a fair estimate. The body has a thousand or two things that could go wrong with it. It is a minutely involved and interrelated system, with nerve centers, muscles, tissues, bones, and a million component parts. Pain is a great conflict creator. Almost anything could go wrong with any of the various systems of the body. It is as susceptible to malfunction as any space ship at Cape Canaveral. If the soul is not capable of absorbing or recycling pain, the human being can be in constant conflict which could last for years or even a lifetime.

For fear that the above might invite a bit of discouragement within you, let me add here words of the great St. Paul who was selected by God to be the first evangelist to the Gentiles at the very early years of the Church. Here is what he says of himself:

"What I do, I do not understand. For I do not do what I want, but I do what I hate. Now if I do what I do not want, I concur that the law is good. So now, it is no longer I who do it, but sin that dwells in me. For I know that good does not dwell in me, that is, in my flesh. The willing is ready at hand but doing the good is not. For I do not do the good I want, but I do the evil I do not want. Now if I do what I do not want, it is no longer I who do it, but sin that dwells in me. So, then, I discover the principle that when I want to do right, evil is at hand." (Rom. 7: 15-21)

It was not God's idea that there be conflicts. He brought our first parents into Paradise. It was their choice to sin that brought on the conflicts that they and all of their posterity had to live under. You can see here how horrible sin must be if it caused, and continues to cause, all of our pain and through pain a tremendous amount of conflict. You may feel justified asking, "What hope is there?" There is hope. Jesus reassures us that, if we believe in Him and follow Him and implement His teaching, a life of peace can be ours, a life in which all conflicts can be melted away. He does not promise that He will take our crosses away but that we will be able to carry them with peace in our souls. If this is true with pain, it must be true with conflicts.

If inner conflicts are not enough, external conflicts can very well be the straw that breaks the camel's back. How much can one human being take? How much do you think that you could take with all that you have to contend within your everyday life? There are those conflicts that arise within the family, within a neighborhood, within a town or village, city, state, country, countries, and within the world. Wars are nothing but swollen conflicts, swollen so much that millions of people are afflicted. You know, and I do too, that it is impossible for you and me as individuals to do too much about external conflicts.

We could do something, but that something is very little when compared to the billions of people engaged in conflict worldwide. Jesus taught us to turn the other cheek, to walk the extra mile. Our Lady pleads for peace, that quality of peace in which all conflict is dissolved. The greatest reason to hope for peace in your life is to realize that you have the Peacemaker abiding within you. It is the Holy Spirit. He is superb in dissolving inner conflicts. If you find that you cannot do much about external conflicts, you might just decide to work on your inner conflicts. Once your inner conflicts are resolved, you will be able to handle external conflicts much better.

Let me share with you what it is that you can do to achieve internal peace. There is still much more that you will learn on your journey about how to come to peace of mind, heart and soul. For now, for a bit of instant relief, enter into a mini-healing session to help ease any conflicts that you may be presently experiencing. I ask you to do the following: Picture yourself on an operating table over which the Holy Spirit has charge. Healing is what He does best. Put yourself under His loving and powerful care. He has all the answers. He knows all the problems. There is no conflict, no matter how great or how long it has lasted, that gives Him the slightest challenge. He has put more souls in order than all psychologists and psychiatrists put together. Give Him your trust. I would recommend that you put the book down for about ten minutes, sit in a comfortable chair or lie down, and ask the Holy Spirit to help you with belief and trust in Him. This is the very first step. Nothing positive happens in healing until there is trust in Him as the Super Healer. When you find that He has put belief and trust into you, ask Him humbly if He would be so kind as to put your soul into a state of quiet for just two minutes. When you do your believing and trusting, do not do so with anxiety. Try it. Take time to do it. If you have to, distance yourself from others so that you can be without distractions. In the meantime, I will be praying that He will give you a little taste of the peace that is His to give. Let's meet at the next chapter in about ten minutes.

CHAPTER 6

Neutral, Neutral, Neutral

"He said to them, 'Come away by yourselves to a deserted place and rest a while.' People were coming and going in great numbers and they had no opportunity even to eat."

(Mark 6:31)

"Come to me, all you who labor and are burdened, and I will give you rest. Take my yoke upon you and learn from me, for I am meek and humble of heart, and you will find rest for yourselves."

(Matt. 11:28-30)

*U*p until now we have been traveling through a mountainous jungle, if you can imagine such a combination. The material has been somewhat deep and "thinky." I am going to ask you to change gears. This is the most important chapter of the entire book. I plead with you, for your own benefit, to take your time with it, to ponder its contents, and to take it to heart.

It will make no sense for you to continue reading unless, at this moment, you are ready to play hard ball. What is coming is not going to be easy. It is going to separate the men from the boys, the women from the girls. You will know now for sure whether you are being selfish, or whether you are expressing love for yourself. There is a vast difference between the two. Either you will grab it for yourself or, out of deep concern for your spiritual welfare, you will give yourself something very, very beneficial to your soul.

If, when I ask you to do what I will ask you to do, you wince and say "No way!" then I recommend strongly that you close this book and give it away. Then get yourself a nice storybook, a good cookbook, or something that will tell you what is new on television, because if you feel that you are not ready to follow the directions presented here, the remaining chapters will do you no good. You see, this book was not written to make you smarter, it was written to make you more holy. I have not written to teach your head, I have written to help you change your heart. What is being asked of you here is what the Lord asked of the rich young man who asked to follow Him: "Go, sell what you have and give to the poor." There is a slight difference, however. I am not speaking here of finances. I am speaking of something that clings to you more than finances.

For what I am going to ask of you, I am absolutely qualified. I have the credentials to prove it. If you do as I ask, I guarantee that you will be a better person, a happier person, and one who will produce much spiritual fruit. If you think that it is too hard, and you turn your back on it as did the young man in the Scriptures, then it will have to be a parting. I have to do what I have to do, and you are free not to do what you feel that you do not wish to do. Let's part friends. You will be in my prayers.

OK, sorry about all that, but what was said had to be said, and now that you have decided to continue on the journey, let's get with it. Time is of the essence. What you have is tremendously important for yourself and for those with whom you live. What I wish of you now is not to read another chapter until and unless you come to NEUTRAL. "NEUTRAL?" NEUTRAL! "But, what does that mean?" It means exactly what you do in your car when you are not in gear, not going reverse or forward. It means that you drop everything, stop everything and just BE. "BE?" BE! That includes to stop THINKING. "THINKING?" THINKING! "IMPOSSIBLE!" No, just difficult.

You see, people are HOOKED on thinking and they don't even know it. That's what is so sad. They don't even know it. "But, what do you DO when you don't think?" Many other things, much more profitable, and much more enjoyable. "Like what?" You will see. Be patient. "BUT, how do you stop thinking? For me it's second to breathing." I will tell you. Be patient.

The first step is to calm down. Let every resistance to life leave you. Right now, for the next five minutes, put yourself into a state where you need to do NOTHING. Pull yourself away from all responsibility, all anxiety, all stress, every bit of ego drive. "Ego drive?" Yes, ego drive. Come to that state of being that the Lord God was talking about when He said, "Be still and know that I am the Lord." (Ps. 46:10)

Softness is the key. Soft heart, soft body, soft head. Just go PLOP. "PLOP?" PLOP! Be like a infant resting in its mother's arms— no fear, no worry, no drive. "BUT, BUT, BUT..." No, buts, just DO it! Close the book, put a marker in your place, and allow yourself for five minutes, to be as an infant in its mother's arms. No ands, ifs, or buts, just DO IT!

AFTER FIVE MINUTES

In trusting that you have taken five minutes, depending on your honesty and sincerity, let's continue. It is obvious that you cannot stop a raging river, at least not easily. Engineers can do it, given the time. What I am asking you to do (and it is not really I, it IS the Lord. He knows how damaging the uncontrolled mind is.), is to take as much will power as you can muster and learn, little by little, to gain access to your mind, to put it into YOUR charge rather than it having charge of YOU. Your mind is to be at YOUR disposal. It was not given to you by God to DOMINATE you. If you continue to be battered by your mind, you will never be free. Never! You will be under the control of what is put into it by the world, the flesh, and the devil.

It is not intended or expected that you gain instant control of your mind. You won't be able to do that. What I am asking of you, however, is to concentrate on putting your will in charge of your mind gradually with patience and especially with the help of the Holy Spirit. It was meant to be that way as decreed by God in His master plan of what a human being was to be and how a human being was to behave.

Again I say: Become the captain of your own ship, the master of your own destiny. If it takes a week, a month, or a year, DO it out of love for yourself and out of obedience to your God. I assure you that your life will change for the better. But, don't put it off. Time IS short. Practice a little everyday.

Learn how to give orders (easy ones) to your mind and make sure that it obeys. Do not give it a second order until it obeys the first. Do not be unreasonable with it, but be tough enough to let it know that YOU are its boss, and it was meant by God to be your worker. The easiest path to follow is to make friends with the Holy Spirit. He is eager to help you. Let Him in on the challenge. Do not try to accomplish this without His help. Doing so will raise your stress level, make you anxious and you will lose rather than gain.

As you learn to be in charge of all of your WHATS, you will become more free and, most of all, better disposed to receive God's graces. There is a deep-rooted yearning within your human heart. It wishes to live a life governed by grace rather than by logic. It wishes to live by the Word of God rather than what is being offered it by the world. This yearning may be buried deep in the recesses of your heart because the daily preoccupations of your life so forcibly swamp it that it does not stand a chance to surface. Nonetheless, it is very real. When you put aside all cares, it will make itself known to you.

It may be shocking for you to know that Satan has our "civilization" by its throat. What he did to our first parents, he is doing now to the whole of mankind. Each one of us is in the Garden of Eden. We have the choice of either looking at God, and doing HIS will or going the way of all flesh. Don't allow yourself to be taken in by the glitter and the enticements of the world. It is all Satan's, and he is making great use of it for his own benefit. The moment of decision is now. Either you put God first in your life, or you will be serving Satan without even knowing it. Need I say more?

The above comes off as being quite abrupt, maybe even a little authoritative. Perhaps so. Nevertheless, it is one prescription that has to be screamed out. Otherwise it will not be paid attention to. Of all the prescriptions you have ever received in your life, I would say that this one is the most important of them all. Take it seriously!

CHAPTER 7

A Glance at Your Mind

"At that time Jesus said in reply, 'I praise You, Father, Lord of heaven and earth, for although you have hidden these things from the wise and the learned you have revealed them to the childlike.' "

(Matt. 11:25)

*T*hank you so much for taking those ten minutes to invite the Holy Spirit to work with your conflicts. You ask," Why should I thank you?" Because you make my work easier and you let me know that you are sincere. You would profit very little if you simply breeze through these chapters. If you were simply to pass from one subject to the other, not too much would stick. I am taking for granted that you really want to learn how to have a fuller life in the use of your head and heart.

By the way, please do not conclude when I invite you to make the journey from the head to the heart, that I am in a way knocking the head. I am not. You will soon observe the great respect and appreciation that is within my heart for the head. The reason why I am absolutely convinced that the journey must be made is the fact that, in our culture, the head has become a god to billions of people. What is being done today all over the world is an ignoring and bypassing of what Jesus, as Redeemer, came on the earth to achieve. In effect, what this book is all about is to be a help to you so that you can reap full benefits from the fruits of that redemption the greatest of which is that of patterning your life after that of Jesus. He came leading with the heart and not with the head. The head has its place in your life and in your redemption, to be sure, but Jesus made it clear by His teaching and by His life that the head is not to have preeminence over the heart. More of this later.

Remind yourself that you were made in the image of God. God IS Mind. God IS Heart. It is the same as saying, God IS Truth, God IS Love. Both truth and love have value, and each must receive its proper respect. The issue at hand is that truth must give deference to love. Truth must be of help to you in order that in the final analysis, your life becomes a life of love. Truth MUST be a stepping stone to love. Truth by itself accomplishes very little. It has great value, don't get me wrong, but its value is always to be directed toward the achievement of a life of love. This is not my teaching. Jesus taught this.

The primary purpose of the mind, as God intended, is to help you to keep searching for Him until you find Him. When your mind is able to present to you that God is lovable, you are ready to shift gears and allow yourself to fall in love with Him. Once you have fallen in love with Him, your next step is to use that love in order for you to give service to Him and through Him to your fellow man. The very fact that the Father sent Jesus into the world, will give you no excuse that you could not find God because you could not see Him or hear Him. God, as God is perfectly reflected in Jesus. Jesus is not difficult to find.

There is another reason why God created you with a mind. He made your mind and gave it to you so that when He wants to speak to you, He can do so "WHAT? God wants to speak to ME?" Of course! Why not?. He speaks to animals, to clouds, to trees. He knows their language. It may interest you to know that they do listen to Him and do EXACTLY what He wants them to do. There are people who may say to you, "God gave you a mind, USE it." All well and good but believe me when I say to you that He leased your mind to you so that HE could use it. As His creature, you belong totally to Him. You are not your own. You are His.

S -o-o-o, your mind is His to use anytime He wants to. Here's the hitch. If you don't want to listen to Him, you could cut Him off, one, two, three. He will never force His Words on you. He made you to be free. He, more than anyone else, respects your freedom. I am sure that you know what it is to call someone on the phone and get a busy signal. You may try for an hour and, if the line continues to be busy, you give up. How about God? He may have been trying to get through to you for years, and for years the only answer He has ever received is your busy signal. If you are using your own mind, He cannot get through to you. He is too much of a "Gentleman" to force Himself on you. He waits, and waits, and waits. That's kind of sad. He can get through to a skunk or a rabbit and yet He cannot get through to you.

The marvels of the mind never cease. God has made it possible to put your mind into a receptive mode. There is more to your mind than just to use it for thinking. It may be a revelation to you to know that you cannot think and listen at the same time. You are either to think, or to listen. If you try to do both at the same time, you create a short circuit. If you, as the heavenly Father's child, would speak to Him as a child (that means, with absolute sincerity), He will not turn a deaf ear to you. If you wish Him to speak to you, He will do so if you really, really listen. I say "really, really," because sometimes we play games with God just to see if He is listening. God does not play games. In the Old Testament there is a reference made to this in a conversation between Eli and Samuel:

"Eli said to Samuel, 'Go lie down and if he calls you, you shall say, "Speak, Lord for thy servant hears."' So Samuel went and lay down in his place. The Lord came and stood forth calling as at other times, "Samuel! Samuel!" And Samuel said, 'Speak, for thy servant hears.'" (1 Sam. 3 9-10)

God can and does speak to us in different ways. He speaks through the Scriptures. He speaks through His Son's Church. He speaks through the prophets. It's best for you not to rule out the possibility that He just may want to speak to YOU directly. It would be in your best interest if, now and then, you would give Him a listening ear.

In addition to thinking and listening, your mind is gifted to do many other things. With it, you can speculate, wonder, evaluate, as in, "Which is better, Advil or Aspirin?" With it you can compose music, write articles, create poetry. It has the quality of creativity. Your mind is able to remember. It is able to recall something that you did ten years ago. It just loves to solve problems. Every minute of its waking day, it wants to know what is new, what's on the agenda. It is curious and is constantly on the watch to see if there is something that it does not know. You can organize your garage by making use of it. It is a tremendous organizer, given the opportunity. It can produce images for you. It is an image maker. Some people call this quality "imagination." This word however has been so flattened out by abuse that I care not to make use of it. At this very moment you could stop and bring up for yourself a mental picture of a schoolmate who, for example, sat in the seat in front of you in math class in first-year high. With the use of your mind you can always be awed, awed by people who cross your path, awed by the clever antics of your cat, awed by God's blessings to you. Who, in their right mind, would ever want to belittle the mind. To do so is unreasonable, unfair, and not very smart. God created the mind and whatever He creates deserves respect.

There was once a philosopher who, a few centuries ago, has done great damage to all of civilization after his time. His name was Descartes. He came up with what he thought was an ingenious statement and turned basic values upside down. What statement could possibly do something as devastating as that? His statement, "I think, therefore I exist." You may have to spend a little time on that one, but it is absolutely ridiculous. He forgot to remember that he was once a child. As a child, he did not as yet enjoy the use of reason. Nonetheless, he DID already exist. What happened with this bit of philosophical nonsense is that it fell right into the ball park of a particular group of philosophers. They used Descartes' statement to put the notion of belief right out of their philosophies. This was the introduction to a variety of philosophies and an educational system based on the lie that if you can't see it, smell it, taste it, hear it, or touch it, it does not exist. What it did was to give science a greater value than the truth that God revealed through Sacred Scripture.

Somewhere along the road of your life, you must have heard the expression: The mind can play tricks on you. It is true because it does have its limitations. On the other hand, as the mind of the soul works through the brain of the body, it is a highly sophisticated bit of creation. Many things can go wrong with it. It can be physically damaged through the brain. It could be psychologically harmed through one's emotional or spiritual type of life. You know well that unless you take good care of your body, a greater or lesser harm can come to it. It is the same with your mind. An improper use of it can cause lasting damage.

5   One of the chief sources of harm to the mind is the fact that it can be allowed to run away with itself. What I mean by this is that if not properly used, the mind could keep on running and accelerating out of control like a runaway engine. It needs the will to keep it in check. If you do not learn to keep your
10   own mind in harness, other people or other things will do it for you and when that happens it will never be to your physical and spiritual advantage. It is you who must be able to say to your mind, "Mind, I don't want you to think about that person. Every time I do, it causes me to have a migraine." It would be
15   most beneficial to you to take charge of your mind. Anytime that you notice that it is zeroing in on something harmful and is riveted to a specific thought or chain of thoughts, it is for your better all-around health and well-being to give your mind a strict order to keep off that particular subject. Your mind
20   needs to be disciplined. It is your will that is in charge of discipline. In this case, as in many others, the mind and the will must work harmoniously together for the health of your entire physical, emotional, and spiritual system. When your mind races and you cannot stop it from thinking, your body and soul
25   lose out because they cannot function properly to maintain themselves in a stable state.

Here is a 'one-liner that will be of great use to you. It is: I AM NOT my mind, I HAVE a mind. If you spend time thinking during all of your waking hours, you can begin to think that
30   doing so is normal and natural, and that's the way life is. It is you as a person who must take charge of your mind's intake. You don't let just anybody or everybody into your home. You should not let just anything or everything into your mind. It is up to YOU to filter whatever presents itself to it. If you learn
35   this, and you can, you will spare yourself high bills and many headaches. It is vital for you to have strength in your will.

Without it, your mind will not listen to you. You will learn more about strengthening of the will, in the following chapter.

Would you like to have another bit of good advice? I knew that you would say yes.

Whether or not you practice the disciplining of your will, will make the difference between the mind serving you or the mind being to you a burden and hindrance. Begin this way: Give yourself the order, not to speak for a minute. Be sure to obey yourself. Then, give your mind an order to think about a particular person. After that, tell your mind to stop thinking for a few seconds. Become aware that willpower is essential for your well-being. Your mind will not respond to your order if you simply internally squeeze your inner head against itself. You cannot force your mind to stop thinking. However, if you give it a bona fide order, one that comes to it from a free and determined will it can learn to listen to the will and even to obey it.

At this point of your journey, you might want to take a little time to practice disciplining your mind. Remember, do not allow yourself to do it with anxiety. Do it in a similar way as a mother when she gives the young child the order, "Do NOT touch the stove. It will burn you." When you get the message across to your mind that it MUST obey you, it will although at the beginning it will still insist on balking. Be patient. Practice makes perfect.

One of the very happy and practical benefits of mental discipline that you will have is that you will sleep well. You will get up each morning well rested. "Why is that?" Because, as you have to admit, when you go to bed and your mind keeps on thinking, without your being able to stop it, your thoughts become worries and you spend much of the night tossing and turning. You might even get up the next morning more tired than you were when you went to bed. As long as the mind is thinking, your physical system has not yet calmed down. Here is a tip. If you learn to fall asleep in your heart, you will sleep well. To fall asleep in your heart means that you fall asleep lovingly, trustingly, or giving obedience to the Lord who does want you to sleep. When you are in your heart, your mind is resting. The greater part of your living experience, is coming forth from the heart. Now, if you watch yourself to see if you are loving, trusting or obeying, it won't work because you are back in your mind again. When little children sleep, they sleep well because they enter into sleep without thought. This is why we have the expression, "I slept like a baby." Check yourself to see if you are trying to sleep and yet find that you cannot stop thinking.. On the other hand, if you concentrate on whether you are thinking, you are still thinking. When you get into bed because God wants you to sleep and you truly and genuinely obey, you will sleep. If you keep on looking into your heart to see if you are obeying, you are thinking and you once again find yourself in the same old rut. Mothers who constantly worry about their children fall easy prey to this. The experience of trusting is the solution. Were a mother to put all of her children into the loving care of Mother Mary, she could drift off to deep sleep trusting that Mary, a good and loving Mother, has everything well in charge. I assure you that what I am sharing with you is the absolute truth. I practice it personally and it WORKS. Before trying this out, go into dry runs while you are still awake. Practice heart activity to put your mind at ease. The entire gamut of heart activity is coming up very soon in one of the following chapters.

One of the greatest boosts that you can give your mind is to put it under the care of the Holy Spirit Who lives within you. He will use it to produce wisdom. He will put knowledge into it which it could not possibly attain by its own natural power. He can so work with your mind that it will come up with an understanding of life, in all of its dimensions, which it could not possibly do on its own. The Holy Spirit can do wonders for your mind. With trust in His power and His love for you, He will surprise you on many occasions and in many different ways as to what spontaneously and without your prompting will come forth. Know enough to be kind to your mind, but don't let it get away with too much.

In conclusion, I would make a gentle suggestion once again that you take a minute or two to exercise your mind with some minor acts of discipline. Test to see if it is your mind, or, if it may perhaps belong to someone else or maybe even to the world at large.

CHAPTER 8

This Is Your Heart Speaking

"And he said: 'Amen, I say to you unless you turn and become like children, you will not enter the kingdom of heaven.'"

(Matt. 18: 3)

"Gross is the heart of this people, they will hardly hear with their ears, they have closed their eyes."

(Matt. 13:15)

*D*o you remember when you bought your last car and you finally got behind the wheel and how exciting it was to try out the new buttons and gadgets on the dash? You tried them all. When you got stuck and could not find what one or the other did, you opened the Owner's Manual and did some research. Well, you and I are going to do something like that right now with regard to your will. I know that your will is not new to you, and maybe you have already experimented with this or that part of it, but I don't think that you have thoroughly gone through it from A to Z. We are going to do that now. Hopefully, it will be in your possession for a good while before the Lord calls you to Himself. So, let us get on with our journey. For this part of it, I need your fullest attention.

You already know that your will was given to you by God when He created you in His image and likeness. You also know that having a will gives you an opportunity to use it. Your WHO uses it as a WHAT. By its very nature, the will seeks out that which is good. It is attracted to goodness. Even should it choose to do some evil thing, it goes for the evil thing because it sees something good in it. It would never reach out for something evil, as evil. What this means is, when a man goes into a hardware store to steal a screwdriver, he may know that it is wrong to steal, but he goes in for the screwdriver because he knows that it will accomplish some good in his using it. As the mind reaches out for that which is true, the will reaches out for that which is good.

What is so singular about your will is that when God created it, He created it to be free. I want you to take a good look at this bit of truth. God, in creating your free will, wanted definitely for you to have a choice between doing what is good and doing what is evil. He gives you the option of doing what He wants of you or doing what you want for yourself. There is even more to it than that. He gave you your free will because as your mind searched for Him and found Him to be lovable, He wanted you to be able to love Him freely and with not even the slightest smidgen of force. Every terrestrial creature under the sun, except man, HAS to do what God wants. It has no choice. You have a CHOICE to do what God wants and, when you do choose to do what He wants, you are able to do it willingly, generously, and with your whole heart.

Many, many people in the world have misinterpreted this freedom, and many, many misinterpret it at this very moment. The nature of the misinterpretation is this: "I am free and I can do anything I want." Again, and for the sake of emphasis, this is not why God made humans free. He made them free so that they would do what HE wants FREELY. Notice once again that the mind with its truth and the will with its freedom must work together. The mind presents the specific truth to the will that it was created free to do GOD'S will. It is the will's responsibility to respond, "OK, I will do it." The consequences of having been born free is that, if you use your will freely to obey God, you will be rewarded by Him. On the other hand, if you use it to disobey Him, you are headed for punishment. No dog is rewarded for being a good dog at least not by God; nor is it punished for being a bad dog, at least not by God.

When one freely chooses to get to know God, the mind comes to the assistance of the will. Once one knows Him and finds Him to be good and lovable, the will gets into action and responds with love and a readiness to give Him obedience. This will give you an inkling why there is so much evil in the world. Our society at large is not using its mind to find God, and therefore understandably, has not found Him to be lovable. It is another indication that the mind must work together with the will. If they work against each other, the will could easily say that it chooses to do whatever it pleases, and so chooses instead not to put itself within the confines of truth, within the confines of what is being presented to it by the mind. You will have to admit that our age is without a doubt the most educated age in history. There have never been more colleges and universities, and yet it becomes evident that something is not quite right. This age enjoys a great level of intelligence and yet suffers from a great depravation of good-ness. Evils have crept right into the educational system, so much so that very often more time is spent in keeping disci-pline than in presenting matter for learning. It is true that the mind must be educated. It must be trained. With the will being left out almost completely by much of the world's inhabitants, what can be expected. The will needs to be discovered, given its due, and put into use.

Just as there is to be a proper training of the mind, there must be a proper formation of the will. This must be from the time of the child's earliest beginning. It must be a formation that comes forth first from the love of its mother. As that little infant experiences within its little nervous system the warmth of love and the comfort of affectionate caresses, it experiences a sense of well-being. Physically and psychologically, it is in a supple and docile condition, ready to be easily molded into a state of goodness. Goodness begets goodness; evil begets evil. As the parents in their goodness are capable of giving good example, goodness attracts the young, and goodness has the potential of being passed from generation to generation. The other side of the coin is that when parents have themselves slipped into a less than virtuous life, this, too, is passed on to their children and grandchildren.

The mind can contain within itself different levels of truth. It can feast on trivia and it can engage itself in considering the deepest of truths. The will also enjoys levels of goodness. You may have experienced times in your own life when you were less good then you are now or even the converse. In the past, you were formed in goodness and wow, look into what you have slipped. The mind can be steeped in error, accepting that which is a blatant falsehood and accepting it as an unques-tionable truth. The will too can accept what is objectively evil and look upon it as a desirable good. Can you see now how both the mind and the will can err, going astray from doing what they are supposed to do by God's design? Let me point out here once again that it is the person who is responsible for the behavior of each of these. God will hold the PERSON accountable for what the mind and the will do.

We could spend hours and days in studying and pondering over what it is that makes the heart evil when it was made by its Maker to aspire after that which is good. The Holy Spirit speaking through the inspired writers of the Scriptures centers many words around what He calls a callous, cold, and hard heart. It brought tears to Jesus' eyes when He found this condition within the hearts of His chosen people. It brings tears to Mother Mary's eyes as she witnesses the same condition in millions of her children in our own times. The Heavenly Father is working every "angle" that He knows in order to bring mankind to a level of goodness. He sent Jesus into the world with His message of and formula for goodness. Despite observing this message and formula exemplified in Jesus' own life, His own generation turned its back on them. Down through the centuries Jesus, continuing His redemptive mission from above, arranged that virtuous men and women be part of every generation. The greater the evil, the more it was supplanted with goodness so as to give an added impetus to human hearts to turn themselves away from that which is evil to that which is good. In a time when goodness seemed to be on the down-swing, Jesus came into the world again in the image of and the devotion to His Sacred Heart. Things did change but only for a brief time. Now, at this very writing, it seems that our Heavenly Father, Jesus, and the Holy Spirit are making what seems to be a last ditch effort to bring mankind to its senses. They, as the Blessed Trinity, are sending Mother Mary into our midst. Jesus has given Mary to be a Mother to all. Knowing that the bond between a mother and her child is the greatest bond known, Mary is being sent as a last resort for humankind to leave its evil and turn to goodness. It balks. Humankind is heading for an unimaginable encounter with God's justice. All of the angels and saints in heaven are praying that men give up their hearts of stone and allow themselves to receive hearts of flesh which are warm, gentle, humble, and loving.

God had known from the beginning the inclination of the human heart to evil, and has been patient and merciful, but He does know how and when to say, "Enough is enough!" He has done so in the past when generations were less evil than what He finds on earth in this our time. The human heart craves to be loved. I think, dear reader, that you know this and experience the truth of it within your own heart. Surely you have become aware of this especially through reports by the media. Many, many evildoers do what they do just to get the attention of others since they are being starved for love and are not able to obtain it in any other way. If you have ever stepped into a mental institution where the element of love is not being experienced, you have seen with your own eyes how the human system becomes fragmented and practically breaks apart. The heart was created by God in order that it would find its true realization in being absorbed by His infinite love. Nothing but being loved infinitely will ever satisfy the deepest cravings of the human heart.

It would be of benefit to you right now if you would recall what was said in one of the previous chapters concerning the importance of every person experiencing self love. Here is the perfect combination which, when found within the human heart, will bring continued fulfillment and genuine and lasting happiness within the person. When you can say from the depth of your own being, "God loves me. I love me. If you don't love me, it's YOUR problem." If all the people in the whole world would love you, it still would not satisfy you. Your heart would still starve somewhere along the way. Your heart MUST experience within itself that it is loved by its Maker. Nothing else will do. You will go on searching and searching until you drop in exhaustion. To know that you are loved by God and to experience that love is the real food that your heart needs so that it can find within itself true and fulfilling peace.

In my own life, I don't think that I have ever seen anything worse than a broken heart. It is at times such as this that I thank God for my priesthood through which He has made me a channel of His healing grace for others. There is a bit of sadness that touches my being every time I go past a junkyard filled with old, dilapidated cars. They are only WHATS. Can you imagine what my heart, and possibly yours, experiences when we see the world full of human wrecks? They are found in every city and town, almost in every family. If you and I, and all human beings on this side of death, could have a peek into the Hearts of the Trinity, into the heart of Mother Mary and of all the saints and angels in heaven, to see how Their hearts must react when they look down upon earth and see the coldness, the ingratitude, and callousness of hearts found in the greater part of the human family, we, too, would shed tears.

As you are allowing your own heart to speak, I hope that you are thankful that you are making this journey from your head to your heart. Hopefully, once you have completed it, you will, with the grace of God, become a full-fledged lover. In becoming so, you could offer a drop of joy to God and His saints. What would bring even more joy to all of heaven is that when you have arrived at the summit of entering into life with a greater love in your heart, you would help just one more person make the same journey. It is refreshing to live in hope. Be it as it may, come, let us move on. The distance for us to travel is still a long one.

CHAPTER 9

Your Heart and
The Experience of Belief

"This is the time of fulfillment. The kingdom of God is at hand. Repent and believe in the gospel."

(Mark 1:15)

"Faith is the realization of what is hoped for and evidence of things not seen. Because of it the ancients were well attested."

(Heb. 11:1-2)

*F*aith, in the broadest sense of the word, is an act of acceptance of a truth from a source that is believable, a source which is other than one's own mind. The source could be one's relatives, friends, historians, teachers, and the like. Faith, in its religious sense, is a gift from God to one baptized wherein the person is capable of accepting all of the truths that God had revealed to mankind from the very beginning of its creation. When that gift is bestowed upon an infant in Baptism, the gift rests within the infant until the it grows old enough to accept it and make use of it for its given purpose. In this chapter, it is this latter form of faith to which attention will be given.

Faith is an experience. It is not a thought. There are those who think "faith" and would conclude that they are believing. Obviously they are wrong. They are actually not believing. Once one has had a genuine faith experience, it becomes clear without the shadow of a doubt that, in fact, faith does come forth from the heart region. The heart region is distinctively different from the head region. Putting it into other words, the mind of your soul works in some mysterious way through the brain. The will of your soul works mysteriously through the heart. It must be concluded, therefore, that though the mind contains the truth to be believed, the basic experience of faith comes forth from the heart. There is a well-defined difference between the experience of thought and the experience of belief. If one has never had a true experience of religious faith, it is easy for such a one to think "faith" and erroneously to conclude that the thought is the real experience. It has to be insisted that it is not.

Perhaps my sternness in the previous chapter can now be better understood and dealt with. In our generation, billions of people are hooked on thought. Most of them do not have the slightest idea that there is more to life. They do have feelings. Thoughts can, and do, provoke feelings. Consequently, most people are governed by feelings rather than by conscience or by any objective norm of morality.

If your nose is as well trained as mine, you too would smell the foulness of Satan. What he is doing, and doing very subtly, is what he did in the Garden of Eden to Adam and Eve. He brought them out of their hearts and tricked them, not only to make the journey from the heart to the head but also to find a comfortable home within the head since they had been convinced by him that there is no better way to live.

If you, dear reader, want to get a handle on this treachery being committed by Satan, begin to exercise discipline over the mind so that it does not run your life. Work to discover the experiences of the heart. There are many. You will notice that, in the coming chapters, the word "experience" is being repeated over and over again, for emphasis sake, to get the point across that to think " trust", to think "love", to think "obedience" is not experiencing what trust, love, and obedience really are. The same can be said of many more virtues. I repeat, there is much more to life than thinking. If you have fallen into the "thinking trap", unless you change your way of life you will become even more enmeshed in the hateful and cunning snares of Satan.

So much rests on having a strong faith. Faith is that virtue which holds up the other virtues. If your faith is weak, so will be the rest of the virtues. Weak faith has been the spiritual ruination of great throngs of people.

There are many reasons for weak faith to show up within a soul. I am firmly convinced that, once the mind begins to tamper with the heart in its maintenance of faith, there comes to be what might be looked upon as a watering-down process. The greater the degree of meddling, the weaker the faith becomes. In addition to this, if the mind is filled with all sorts of thoughts that are inimical to the faith maintained in the heart, additional damage is done to one's faith. When the mind begins to question matters of faith and begins to enter-tain doubts, that too causes harm. When the mind becomes so preoccupied with matters of the world, matters which contribute to a self-oriented life, faith is quick to fade away. It would seem to me that faith is lost by degrees correlative to the degrees of greater and greater interference in that which is still held on to by the heart. With no interference by a world-oriented head, the person grows in faith; but the more interference by the world-oriented head, the weaker becomes the person's faith. Remember well that each person who has been gifted with faith has the responsibility of safeguarding it and growing in it.

The mind is not the only culprit in the lessening of and even to the actual loss of faith. The heart itself can do damage to the faith that is within it. When the heart begins to pay attention to the mind and goes out to that which is offered by the mind, the heart does damage to its own faith. If there is a gradual easing away from virtue and a more and more frequent gratification of one's carnal desires, faith is put aside and ignored. What follows is: There is a lessening of faith to the degree that one eventually loses it. There are many causes for the lessening and loss of faith, too many to mention. Faith has to be nurtured, has to be practiced. Acts of faith need to be made. If there is a general slackening of effort to be virtuous, the inevitable happens.

There are various indications in the behavior of a person that faith is being put on the back burner, or at least on hold. When the prayer life is neglected and time spent in prayer is gradually lessened to a minimum and finally completely ignored, the danger flag is up. When Mass attendance becomes mechanical and occasionally missed with no great reason, that is a sure sign that evil is setting in. When an illicit attachment headed for an involvement surfaces, faith begins to become secondary. Unexpected riches, popularity and power can do a number on one's quality of faith. When the line "I don't practice my religion as I used to." comes up, it is an indication that one has illicit attachment to things of the world instead of the most important thing in the world — faith.

The moral thermometer of the world is, degree by degree getting close to the freezing point. When you have one rotten apple in a bushel of apples, the health of the good apples is not seriously threatened. With each additional rotten apple, the chances that the rest of the bushel will survive rot is slim and, finally, the entire bushel has to be discarded. No one today will say that the world is getting better and better. There are many who with valid convictions are saying that the world is getting worse and worse, more and more evil. The greater the evil, the weaker the faith. Our Lord made a shocking statement concerning the world and faith. "I tell you, he will see that they get justice, and quickly. However, when the Son of Man comes, will he find faith on the earth?" (Luke 18:8) The very fact that faith is at such a low ebb in the world would almost be a sure indication that the Son of Man will be coming soon.

The loss of faith in the world at large is one thing, the loss of faith within the Catholic Church is quite another. The world does not have the sources of strengthening faith as has the Church. Jesus had put all of the necessary ingredients into His Church to assure its survival to the end of the world. The Mass, the Eucharist, the Sacraments, the leadership of the Holy Father, the devotions, and many other aids to maintain and even strengthen it, are available to every Catholic man and woman. The Second Vatican Council was convened for many special reasons and especially to bring the Faith into the world for its evangelization. What happened, by demonic design, I believe, was that the world entered into the Church instead. The great apostasy made mention of in Scripture is upon us. The number of clergy, religious, and lay people who have left the Church in the last thirty years is without precedent. The lessening of reverence within God's House, the confusion among the laity, the lack of leadership on the part of some of our shepherds, the tampering with Sacred Scripture, the games which the theologians are playing, all of these reflect a lack of faith and bring heartaches and tears to the faithful remnant.

Mind you, I am not saying that Vatican II caused all this. I do wish to point out that Second Vatican Council, convoked by the Holy Spirit was just what the world needed. What then went wrong? Plain and simple. Those who implemented the decrees failed to send through the Church the genuine conclusions of the Council. This happened especially with the liturgical conclusions which were given to upgrade the faith of the people of God. Those responsible for bringing about liturgical reform failed in the trust that had been placed upon them.

It was mentioned above, in connection with the subject of lessening and loss of faith, that being with the world is one thing, but being with the Church is quite another. Now, let us turn this around: With the CHURCH is one thing, but with the world is something else. I say this because, with the Church there is still hope; with the world there is none. Do remember that the Holy Spirit is in charge of the Church, Mary is its Mother and St. Joseph is its protector. With that combination, the Church will not only survive, but thrive. When the Pharisees of old witnessed Christ on the cross, bending His Head in death, they left elated by victory. Christ's Church will follow pattern. Its enemies who have infiltrated not only the sanctuary but its highest summit, will come to a point, when they will say, "We DID it." When Jesus rose from the dead, His enemies turned red with rage. When the present enemies become convinced that the Church is dead, they too will rejoice but not for long. It will be brought out of limbo with a life more resplendent than ever in its history. This day is not far off.

We have saved the best for last. What might that be? The numbers are few, as Jesus reminds us, "For many are invited, but few are chosen." (Matt. 22:14) Within the hearts of some of the faithful, there is already the evidence of a Springtime of an enlivened and inflamed faith. The externals may look bleak, as in the months March and April in our northeast, but look to the base of the plants and bushes — a new rich green evidence of life is already there. The greater the evil, the greater the amount of grace that heaven sends upon earth. There are evidences upon evidences that the faith within the bowels of the Church is as strong as ever and is becoming stronger by the day. Dear reader, there IS hope.

In conclusion, how can YOUR faith be strengthened? The list is rich and long. The greatest "strengthener" of faith is the Holy Spirit. He has more ways than one can count to bring you to a new height of vibrant faith. He is working within the hearts of millions of souls. Each one is being treated uniquely. Each receives a singular, custom made prescription. All you have to do is to say with sincerity of heart, "Holy Spirit, I believe, help my unbelief," and presto it's done. It is not necessary nor advisable to check to see if He has done as requested. The mind is not the one that has an accurate measuring tape. The answer to that prayer will be found in an improvement in your prayer life and in the added selflessness which will be yours in the performance of kind deeds. Make friends with the Holy Spirit. Treat Him with reverence and trustingly leave your growth in faith within His loving embrace.

Prayer, prayer with the heart, is enormously helpful. Participating daily at the Sacred Liturgy is excellent. Spending time with Jesus in the Blessed Sacrament will provide bushels of spiritual vitamins. Make acts of faith by slowly and sincerely going through each part of the Apostles' Creed. A devout recitation of the rosary is high on the list. Living the faith on a day-to-day basis, living on the outside that which faith expresses on the inside, is a sure sign of growth. Forming prayer groups and/or joining one already in existence has helped hundreds of thousands to grow stronger in faith. Reading the Scriptures, especially the Gospels, is a sure way to obtain added spiritual strength — if read with faith. Making an effort to perform loving acts to those in need is sure to draw down from heaven a bolstering of one's faith. Again, I repeat, put yourself under the powerful care of the Holy Spirit. Become docile to His nudges and prompts. That's the best. Your growth in faith will take time and require effort, maybe even sweat and blood, but so what. The resulting dividends will be worth all that.

In the days of the Baltimore catechism, it was required of all to learn the Act of Faith by heart. Let me share it with you for your own edification. I don't say that you have to memorize it, but capture its essence and make it in your own words.

"Oh my God, I firmly believe that You are one God in three Divine Persons: Father, Son, and the Holy Spirit. I believe that Your Divine Son became Man and died for our sins, and that He will come to judge the living and the dead. I believe these and all the truths which the Holy Catholic Church teaches, because You have revealed them, Who can neither deceive nor be deceived. Amen."

It would not be fitting to conclude this chapter on faith without a plea for prayer for those who are in spiritual trouble, for those intent on spiritual suicide. I am thinking especially of the some of the leaders within the Church. It would seem almost contradictory for the lay people to give assistance to the clergy and to the hierarchy, since the primary responsibility of the clergy and the hierarchy is to give assistance to the laity. Nonetheless, remember that if there is one demon sitting on the roof of every house to do spiritual harm to its inhabitants, there are at least fifty demons sitting on the top of every rectory. They know full well that if they can get a priest to fall, it's like the enemy capturing the general of an army. It should be a great incentive for you to pray for the priests and bishops when you recall the following frightening words of Jesus. "But if anyone causes one of these little ones who believe in me to sin, it would be better for him to have a large millstone hung around his neck and to be drowned in the depths of the sea." (Matt. 18:6)

Here is a final little prescription. Take a minute or two before going to the next chapter to express a hearty "thank you" to Jesus for your faith. His suffering and death earned it for you. May the Holy Spirit help you to share it with others by way of your words and your deeds. They will be eternally grateful to you.

CHAPTER 10

Your Heart and the Experience of Trust

*"Do not let your hearts be troubled.
Trust in God, trust also in Me."*
(John 14:1)

*"Notice how the flowers grow.
They do not toil or spin. But I tell you,
not even Solomon in all his splendor
was dressed like one of them. If God
clothes the grass in the field that
grows today and is thrown into the
oven tomorrow will He not much
more provide for you, O you of
little faith!"*
(Luke 12:27-28)

*T*rust, when spoken of as a human quality, is an experience of the heart wherein is expressed surrender to another who has been found trustworthy. It means that by my previous association with you, I am able to trust you because by your attitude and behavior; you have proved yourself worthy of my trust. Because I found you to be sincere, because I witnessed your goodness, I freely chose to give up my guard and allow what you say about me and do to me to be acceptable. I am not afraid that you will either lead me astray by what you say to and about me or that you will harm me in any way by what you do to or for me. I am at ease in your presence. In fact, I enjoy spending time with you.

Human trust is a laudable quality. It is not, however, the form of trust that we intend to focus on within this chapter. The particular trust with which we will spend time is the supernatural or superhuman kind referred to as the theological virtue. The heart practicing the theological virtue of trust focuses its entire attention on God.

When you were young in faith, you spent time learning the acts of faith, hope, and charity. You will remember in the previous chapter, I referred to faith as belief. I will now refer to hope as trust, and in the following chapter, instead of using the word charity, I will use the word love because the words faith, hope, and charity have been somewhat watered down and flattened out through modern usage. For example, someone might say that he hopes that tomorrow will be a nice day for a picnic. This usage of hope is entirely different from the meaning of hope in the context of a relationship with God. Were I to say that I HOPE in you, you do not get the clear message as if I were to say that I TRUST in you.

One of the greatest and most exciting acts that the human heart is capable of is this very same experience of trusting God. If you really and truly were to put your complete trust in God, you would enjoy a peace that is truly out of this world. It is the peace that Jesus spoke of when He mentioned the peace that the world cannot give. This peace is a reward from

God for trusting. He gives the reward because when you trust Him without reservation, without strings attached, you are expressing an excellence in your behavior that is most pleasing to Him. This is so because, by trusting Him, you are fulfilling one of the very purposes for which He made you.

What makes this trust so special is that it is a gift from God. It was given to you at the time of your Baptism as were also belief and love. Consider this: God gives you the gift of trust so that you can trust Him; and trusting Him, you can accomplish one of the purposes for which you have been put on earth. It is not everyone who can put trust in God. As with the theological virtue of belief, trust was given to you at the moment of Baptism in "seed" form. It could not be used by you because, as an infant, you were not yet developed enough to be able to make use of it. It was to sprout within you during the time of your religious formation when you were old enough to understand what it was and, especially, when you matured enough to make use of it.

This trust in God becomes very active once you begin to have an idea of just Who God is. Should your knowledge of God be simply intellectual, trusting Him would not automatically follow. As a heart expression, you need to be living a life in the heart to be able to appreciate trust for what it is. The mind can get to know ABOUT God. This knowledge of Him intellectually cannot trigger trust since the mind is incapable of bringing the heart into action. Once you know God personally, that is a different matter. Getting to know God person to person, brings your heart close enough to the "Heart" of God to be able to elicit an act of trust.

This is one of the reasons, among others, that the Father sent Jesus into our midst, just so that we could get to know God as He is. Jesus is the Son of God and is also referred to as the Word. He is incarnate, becoming like you, so that with your human attributes, you could relate to Him, Who, in a visible form makes it easy enough for you to get to know exactly what God the Father is like. Falling in love with Jesus, is falling in

love with God. Jesus is God and Man. As such, He forms a bridge between God and you. Jesus' coming into our midst is a tremendous gift on the part of the Father, a gift that expresses itself in many, many ways. Once you can find through Jesus,
5   that God is lovable, you will more easily be able to leave behind trust in yourself for that which is more rewarding, namely, trust in God. Because of the superior qualities found in God, it becomes reasonable to leave self and go to God in total trust.

10   When you were three or four years of age, you would not think of crossing a four-lane highway on your own, even at a crossroad. But putting your little hand into the hand of your father, you would strut across without the least amount of fear, simply because you were with your father whom you trusted
15   even though your little head knew nothing of what it meant to trust. You just did it because of who you were, a helpless tot, and who your father was, one who could do anything. You placed yourself into his care without even thinking.

It is the very same way with you and God. God is God, and
20   you are you. You know full well that you have limitations. You know that you cannot handle every facet of life. You have become aware of His divine powers, powers that you do not have, powers that you need to have to live, powers that God freely and joyfully shares with you. Jesus presents Himself to
25   you as your loving Brother who loves you without strings attached, who wishes you the most and the best. He gives to you lovingly and generously, whatever it is that you need to attain your goal in life — the salvation of your soul.

God is not only your Creator, but He is your Father. As a
30   human father provides for the needs of his children, so the Divine Father provides for His children in ways that the human father cannot. This is not to be taken as a slur. It is a fact. Earth is earth, heaven is heaven; human is human and divine is divine. As the human father takes the initiative in the care of
35   his children, God, the Father, does the same. He needs not to be asked. He knows your needs better than you do. There may

be times when the child asks his father for something that is unreasonable, something that is not a genuine need. The father does reply that he cannot do what he is being asked to do. There is nothing that God, the Father, cannot do. However, His Wisdom prevents Him from acquiescing to one or the other of your requests because, what you are asking of Him is not good for your physical or spiritual welfare. The deeper your trust in God, in the Father's loving concern for you, the less you feel the need to ask Him for anything. Your trust can become so deep that your entire human system goes through life on a day-to-day basis without fear. There is something inside of you that makes it possible for you to glide along in life without the slightest worry. It is a quality that is so liberating, so invigorating, that you can afford to put all defenses down and disengage yourself from all resistance to God in the things that He asks of you. Life, in this valley of tears takes on a brand-new dimension broadening your vision, filling in the deep potholes, and bringing down to size what before were unattainable heights. Your total trust in God makes your life not only tolerable but even a life filled with joy despite pains, setbacks, and heartbreaks.

Father, you say, you are dreaming. I cannot possibly trust God that much. I am a mere struggling Christian trying to save my soul by doing such things as being obedient to the Commandments, the Precepts of the Church, and whatever conscience demands of me. You must be talking to someone whom you think to be a saint. Maybe yes, maybe no. What I am pointing out to you is that this quality of trust has been implanted within your heart. It is there for you to make use of. It is only for you to accept in your heart that the Holy Spirit began His dwelling within you with trust. All that remains for you to do is to use it. Somewhere in your prayer books you will find an Act of Trust. An example of such an act is the following:

"O my God, relying on Your Almighty Power and Infinite Mercy and Promises, I trust to obtain pardon of my sins, the help of Your grace, and life everlasting through the merits of Jesus Christ my Lord. Amen"

If you refuse to just to think these words, but instead put your heart into them, you predispose yourself to the Power of the Holy Spirit Who will make these words real. Know that there is hope for you by remembering that the Holy Spirit is the Sanctifier. It is true. Your purpose in life is to become a saint. Jesus, too, takes your side when He says to you: "For nothing will be impossible for God." (Luke 1:27)

It has to be admitted that, in our culture, trust is difficult to come by either on the human or on the supernatural level. You are paddling your boat upstream against the flow of the current. It is once again a case of distancing yourself from the influence of others. Put your nose to your own grindstone. Plod ahead doing what you know that you should do. You gain nothing by spending your life bouncing off other people. Plot your own course. In prayer, zero in on what it is that God expects of YOU and let the sparks fly where they may. Call to mind once in a while that when your time is up and you are standing before the Lord in judgement, you will be responsible for your own behavior not the behavior of other people. Demand of yourself to be enough of an individual that you do what is best for you. Make an effort to be more trusting in God. Live a life of trust in God no matter what others are doing. Help is always within you. All that is necessary is a sincere request: "Holy Spirit, help me to grow in trust of You, of Jesus, of the Father, of all the angels and saints." Don't merely think the words, let your heart speak them directly and don't watch your heart as it is reaching out in need to its God.

Pride fights trust and wants to live without it. Take it from this old man. I have for years worked on this very quality of trust. All my efforts proved to be in vain until I happily stumbled on the real Holy Spirit. I said "real" because I knew of Him theologically for years and years. The real Holy Spirit is found within the recesses of the heart. In exasperation and even in the depth of desperation, I said, "Holy Spirit, you HAVE to help me. I have no other place to turn. I had tried everything to grow in trust. The harder I tried, the worse it got. I will risk trusting that You will help me with my trust. I dump (not a very nice word, but that's the only one that really fits) myself into Your care. I give up trying. If You can't help me, no one else can. Help me to trust in You enough to be able to ask you to increase my trust." It worked because I finally meant business.

Be patient with yourself. As I mentioned to you earlier, put your mind into a harness. Take charge of it and demand that it stop coming up with excuses to trust.

What really helped me was when I opted to live more by experiences rather than by mere thoughts. You will not find any trust in thoughts. You will find also that putting your full trust either in yourself or in other humans postpones a genuine liberation. Trusting the Holy Father is one exception. He is himself under the influence of the Holy Spirit especially when speaking officially to the whole Church on matters of faith and morals. When he speaks thus, he speaks not for his own benefit but for yours and that of the whole believing Church. This is what is meant when it is said that the Holy Father speaks infallibly. Even in other areas he can be trusted. Yes, he is human but as the Vicar of Christ, the Successor of St. Peter, he receives extra help from the Holy Spirit so as to keep the Flock from going astray.

In conclusion, allow me to share with you an experience that basically helped dramatically to change my life for the better. It took place when I was in Assisi on a sabbatical some years back. I had trouble controlling my emotions. I pleaded with the Spirit to help me. Internally, I carried on a conversation with Him using no external words. He made it clear to me that He would help me provided that I would do exactly what He prompted me to do. I said I would. He asked me for the next three days not to think of the past. I did with as much will as I could muster up. After three days, I reported and got an A+. This was followed by the directive that for the next three days I was not to think of the future. This I did. It was a bit more difficult than working with the past but, with the help of God, I succeeded. I received only an A. Then, for the next three days, I was not to think of myself. That was tough, tougher than you can imagine. I failed badly the first three days. I was told to work on it for three more. With sweat and blood, I made it, barely obtaining a C.

All this hard work was extremely tiring. I asked for a few days off in order to rest. It was granted. When I reported back for further instructions, He dropped a bombshell. "For the next three days, you may obey me as your God but you may not think of me," He said. I was absolutely devastated. I could not think of the past. I could not think of the future. I could not think of self. I could not even find relief in putting my thoughts on God. This was agony. I kept my promise to obey. It was one of the most difficult things I ever went through. But then came one more request. "Now," He said, "you may not think about not thinking." He brought my mind right to a halt. When He did, I was led into an experience I had not had since my child-hood days. I came to the experience of "BEING." I didn't think. I didn't feel. I just "BE'D." It was indeed the most rewarding experience I ever had in my entire life. I was able to spend hours, even days in just "being."

Then, all heaven broke loose. When my mind was put to rest, my heart came forward in a life that I never imagined possible. I believed, trusted, loved, forgave, was grateful, thankful and was reverent as never before in my whole life. I renewed my vows to the Lord better and with more generosity than when I made them for the first time. I experienced freedom and like the angels and saints in heaven, I believed. I understood for the first time what Jesus meant when He said, "When you lose your life, you will find it."

I do acknowledge that you could not take a sabbatical and give up three weeks to obtain the same experience. Nevertheless, work somewhat in the same fashion to curb the unruly power of your mind. If you allow your mind to be your dominant tool in life, it will sell you short. If you would dare to make a leap in faith to the very same Holy Spirit Who was so good to me, He would be happy to give you a crash course. As you continue reading the coming chapters, you will find that there will be one item that will appear again and again. It is to plunge into the heart and let it be the base from which you do all things. It will be like being in a motorboat, going full steam ahead, with the motor governing the boat from behind. Once the battle for the preeminence of the heart is behind you, you will have believing thoughts, loving thoughts, forgiving thoughts, trusting thoughts, and on and on. Take my word for it that once the mind becomes second in your life, it will be opened up in such a way that it will serve you better than ever. The Holy Spirit will just flood it with thoughts that you could not possibly ever come to on your own. Once you are able to clear your mind of earthy thoughts, the Spirit will fill you with thoughts that will make you think that you died and were in heaven. You will never believe the wisdom, the knowledge, the understanding that will be yours. In addition, you will enjoy peace of mind, peace of heart, and peace of soul — all because of your life of trust and putting all of your eggs in God's basket, putting all of your cares and worries into His loving care.

Why not take five before diving into the next chapter. Spend a few minutes trusting that you could trust God. Do this first on a trial basis. Once He proves Himself trustworthy, you might want to do it on a lifetime basis. You will be able to handle the coming events better if you start practicing to trust God without putting it off.

CHAPTER 11

Your Heart and the Experience of Love

"I give you a new commandment: love one another. As I have loved you, so you should love one another."
(John 13:34)

Jesus answered and said to him, 'Whoever loves Me will keep My word, and My Father will love him, and We will come to him and make Our dwelling with him.'"
(John 14:23)

*T*here is no greater or more perfect expression of life on earth or in heaven than love. It is no wonder that this is so, since the source of all life is God and God IS Love. Love is not simply one of His descriptive attributes which would come under human perception as an adjective. We know that God is all powerful and all knowing. It would not be correct to say that God is all loving except by default of our human understanding. Love, when speaking of it as pertaining to God, is a noun. Love is what God IS. It is not what God HAS or what God DOES. It is what God IS. God is Love by His very nature, by His very essence, by His very existence. Everything that has come forth through His creative power has come into existence because of His love. Everyone who has been created by Him, in His image and likeness, has not only been created in love but to love as well.

If it is so that everything and everyone has been created by God in love, how is it that there are crocodiles, mosquitoes, and poison ivy? How is it that hatred is found among angels and human beings? As far as the former, God would not have created these except out of love and for some definite good that scientists have not yet been able to determine. As far as the latter, God in His love, sharing with them the best He had, gave human beings a free will. Those who chose not to share in His love distance themselves from Him. Hatred is the absence of love. The farther away parts of the earth are from the sun, the less they benefit from its warmth. So too, the more one hates, the more one is distanced from the Son of God; conversely, the more one distances one's self from God, the less one benefits from His loving warmth. Satan and his devils turned one hundred and eighty degrees from God and did it freely, instantly and completely. They are totally devoid of love. Theirs is hatred through and through. They are hateful persons. Human beings, through Adam and Eve, also distanced themselves from God but in a lesser way. These are given another opportunity to enter back into love through the coming of the Messiah, Jesus Christ, true God and true Man.

If Jesus had come into the world to reinstate mankind into God's love, how is it that there is still hatred in the world? It is because human beings have a free will and, despite the fact that they have been given an opportunity to reinstate themselves, there are those who choose not to. There are human beings on earth who love. There are those who hate. Those who personally draw close to Christ are they who are loving. Those far away from Him are they who are hateful. The human condition is not as clear-cut as stated. To treat it in depth would take another volume.

You may have heard that love is a many splendored thing… and so it is. However, the word love has a variety of meanings in our day. Speaking of the love of God is one thing; speaking of that which some humans call love is another. True love is a spiritual quality. It comes from the soul. It is found in the will, that is, in the heart. What some call love is not love at all. Rather, it could be a physical reaction at the sight of beauty in the human body. It could be that particular experience that is had through the arousing of the sexual passion. It could be an emotional feeling known as "puppy love." It could also be other things too many to consider now. Out of fairness, however, it should be mentioned that there is a valid human love just as there is a valid human trust. Human love would be more self-oriented than the love that we will be considering. The content of what will be discussed here will be the love that is a gift from God to a baptized person. It is love that has God as its object. It is love at its best, the theological virtue.

True spiritual love, the highest form of love that a human being can experience, comes from the love that the Holy Spirit infused into the human heart at the time when He took up His dwelling within a soul at the time of Baptism. Spiritual love perfects the natural love that is already in the human heart through God's act of creation. It must be cultivated in the same way as belief and trust. It is activated when there begins to be an awareness of the presence of the Holy Spirit as at the reception of Jesus at one's first Communion and at Confirmation.

The Act of Love taught to the young in preparation for the reception of these Sacraments is helpful to all who make use of it. For your benefit, here is what it contains:

"O My God, I love You above all things, with my whole heart and soul, because You are all Good, and worthy of all my love. I love my neighbor as myself for the love of You. I forgive all who have injured me, and ask pardon of all whom I have injured. Amen."

The prayer is short but to the point. When this act is repeated, and truly said from the heart, the Holy Spirit gives an increase of this supernatural virtue. A sincere desire to grow in love, to become more loving, makes it easier for Him to do His work.

What I say now bears repeating. It is not thinking love that is the experience of love. The more undisciplined is one's mind, the less capable is one of expressing this love. The mind must be made to slow down and even come to a halt. Unless this happens, love is never given the opportunity to express itself fully. For one's well-being, love needs to be able to fill the whole soul to make it possible for the Holy Spirit to establish Jesus' kingdom within it. When love permeates the mind, the mind takes on a new dimension. The mind becomes even more vibrant when it is impregnated with love. It becomes less judgmental, less critical, and is better able to find goodness in others. It is this that makes it possible for one to enjoy peace of mind.

To love can be a matter of choice, it can be a matter of obedience. Of course, we can and should choose to be obedient. The choice in favor of obedience is also a choice to love. Here is what the Lord God says, "You shall love the Lord, your God, with all your heart, with all your being, with all your strength and with all your mind, and your neighbor as yourself." (Luke 10:27) You are given the option of wanting to love or having to love. Surely there is a difference between choosing freely to live these two commandments or having to obey them by obligation. The difference in plain language comes out clearly when you say, "I want to love God." or "I have to love God." You can put that combination together were you to say, "I want to obey to love God." In any event, this is what you are being asked to do with the love that the Holy Spirit implanted into your heart. It is not to be only a warm loving feeling. God intends for each of us to put this love into good service.

In loving God with your whole being you choose to put Him first in your life. You center your life around His wishes. One other expression of your love is experienced by the gift of yourself to God. God has given each of us to ourselves and hopes that we would freely admit that we really belong to Him and that we would freely choose to give ourselves back to Him. In this gift of self to God, He accepts you and, in turn, gives Himself to YOU. Who gains? You do. You give yourself to Him with all of your limitations and failings and He gives Himself to you with all of His perfection. This is not a game. This is true love.

When you give yourself to Him, you create a sort of vacuum. You empty yourself of yourself so that there is room for God to enter into you. When this happens, He elevates you to a new life, a supernatural life. He fills you with HIS love. As a result, you now love with the love of Jesus, or more accurately, Jesus uses your heart to make your heart express perfect love.

The above exchange of gifts is the same as what takes place in the Sacrament of Matrimony. He says to her, "Honey, I'm YOURS." She, in turn, says to him, "And, Sweetie Pie, I'm YOURS." It is precisely in this gift of one to the other that the bond of love "glues" them into being "one." When this is expressed daily in their life together, with the grace of the Sacrament, there is the guarantee that they will be together bonded in love "till death do us part." Consider this! Once the mind begins to interfere in this mutual gift of self, and she begins to find fault with him, and/or he begins to analyze her behavior, the "glue" begins to thin out. As long as they continue freely and generously to give themselves to each other and the mind is trained through the heart not to interfere, the love between them grows, and grows, and grows.

Suppose now that each of the above partners, being baptized and living under the influence of the Holy Spirit, carried on a life relationship with God together and on an individual basis. She gives herself in love to God; he gives himself in love to God, and God enters into each of them and raises their individual lives to a divine level. Can you see what joy there would be in such a marriage? Wishful thinking? No! I have personally met couples bonded to each other and each bonded to their God. What a blessing for their children, and their children's children! Such a bond with each other and each with God makes it possible through the ups and downs of life, different personalities, different temperaments, different backgrounds, for their love to bond so thoroughly that they truly become one. Instead of being thwarted by setbacks, these bring them even closer together.

Not all the blame for the lessening of and/or the disappearance of love between husband and wife should be directed to the critical and analytical mind. There is the infamous trio of the world, the flesh and the devil. The world with its attractions and enticements caters to the gratification of the individual making it difficult for each to leave self in favor of the other. The flesh, stimulated by what is offered by the sex saturated culture, tends to look for its own fulfillment at the expense of the other. Satan, the master dis-unifier, takes every possible occasion to pit one against the other. If it were not for the graces that flow from the Sacrament to bolster marital love, the divorce rate, as high as it is, would climb even higher. It is the Love of the Spirit that abides within the hearts of those married, that gives continued courage to loving couples despite all of the attacks against harmony and fidelity in marriage. It is tapping into the Sacrament that assures that one's marriage remains sacred.

Who in today's world would be willing to give one's self totally, totally to God? There are some. To offer this gift of self to God is nothing that should be considered heroic. You did not make yourself. It would stand to reason that if you did not make yourself, you were made by Someone. You know that already. To put it in a slightly different way, you do not own yourself. You belong to the One Who created you. Is that not true? So, if you say to God from your heart, "God, you gave me life. I owe my life to you. I belong to you. I am yours." Why is it not heroic to admit this and to follow through on it? It is because it is simply the truth. To acknowledge that something is the truth, if it is the truth, should be the simple matter of accepting it as the truth. Once accepted, the heart is able to follow through. It would be considered heroic today because there is such a gap between head and heart that anyone who makes the effort to bridge the gap and bring the truth of the heart in tune with the head has much work to do repairing the damage done by our culture of the mind. Your hearty statement to God, "God, I am yours, so I give myself to you," would bring your life into the fullness of truth. From within that state you would derive abounding physical as well as spiritual benefits.

Before the truth can be lived, one must first believe — believe in God. Considering it on a personal level, you must believe that God exists and that He created you in His image and likeness. It demands that you get to know Him for Who He is. It would follow that from this state of belief you would pass on to a trust in this God Who, out of love for you, brought you into life. When trust in God fills your soul, the final step is not difficult. You could very easily say, "God, I trust You so much, I trust you enough to put myself into Your care. I give myself to you to do with me whatsoever you choose." A good clear head would accept the logic of this; a heart with good will would jump to put it into practice. So much for the first great Commandment of loving God completely with your whole being with all that it implies.

Now for the second. You are being asked by God to love your neighbor as you love yourself. If you love yourself, it will be no problem for you to love your neighbor. But, do you REALLY love yourself? Do you love yourself enough to give yourself the best that life has to offer? What might that be? It is the chance to enjoy total happiness for all eternity.

If your mind is of twentieth-century vintage, it probably has at least thirty reasons why you should not love yourself. If you have learned to bypass your mind and enter into your believing heart, you would neutralize the thirty reasons by one single act of belief. This would come out of you as, "God loves me, so why should I not love myself." If He accepts me "as is," as He makes it clear in many ways that He does, then I am relieved. Consequently, I can go on to obey the second part of the Commandment. It would then make sense to me to be able to say: "I love my neighbor because I love myself. I love myself because God loves me."

To be loved is the number one craving of the human heart. It is not satisfied by the love of many. It is not fulfilled by quantitative love. Its craving goes much deeper than that. It wants to be loved infinitely. It wants to be loved by its Owner Who, too, is Infinite. It is He, Who in creating you, put that craving into your heart so that you would ultimately join Him. Happiness would be yours because you would be fulfilling your primary purpose in life.

The little catechism question and answer comes to mind. Q. "Why did God make you?" A: "God made me to know Him, to love Him, and to serve Him, and to be happy with Him for all eternity." Have you any idea of what God waits to hear from you, from your person, making use of your whole being, heart, mind, body and soul? It is your permissive statement, "God, you may love me." Love cannot ever be forced on another. God knows that. He will never force His love on you. He waits patiently, sometimes for years, for you to give Him the green light.

Were you to put your finger on the one thing that is wrong with our generation, where would you put it? Take time to think. I can give you an inkling. It's that we, as people, are never satisfied. This is the whole bag of worms that is daily opened in front of us, as soon as we open the morning paper or flip on the news. There are degrees of dissatisfaction, some are more dissatisfied or less dissatisfied, but every one of us, with very few exceptions, lives in a state of dissatisfaction. In searching for satisfaction, there are those who are ready to kill and do so. There are those who stop at nothing or no one to attain power and riches, even if they have to climb over thousands, and sometimes, millions, of people to get these. The solution of our ills can be resolved by one hearty statement, "God, You may love me."

If you love God, you will love Jesus, or more accurately, if you love Jesus, you will love God. If you love God, you will love the angels, all the saints and especially the Father's fairest Daughter. You will love every person in the world in as much as every person, like yourself, is created in the image and likeness of that God Whom you love. You will love the Church, as the Mystical Body of Christ, you will love the Eucharist because it is Jesus living in our midst. You will love sinners because God loves them. You will love the Gospels because they contain the words and life of Jesus. In allowing God to love you, you will be filled with not human, but divine, love and you will love with His love all that He loves. If you let God love you, you in turn will become a bona fide lover. As God IS Love, you will be an expression of that love for all eternity.

There are times, if you are like everyone else, you run low on love; in fact you might run right out of it. God knew that would happen so He set up a Love Station. "LOVE STATION?" Yes, you know, just like a gas station when you need gas. The Love Station is the Mass. If only our people of the Faith would know this, they would be cramming their parish churches to wall-to-wall capacity. Let's spend a little time with this "Love Station" concept.

The Mass, by definition, is the Unbloody Continuation of Jesus' Death on the Cross. What is it that He did on that Cross? He gave Himself in total love to His Father in our behalf. That includes you and me. He paid a bill to our Father we could not possibly pay. You and I were not at the foot of that Cross when Jesus did this. Because He came for the benefit of all people, He arranged that everyone in all of the centuries till the end of time, could come to the foot of that Cross in a mystical way. There IS a real death that takes place in your presence as you participate at Mass. It is a mystical death, a death that has reality. This is how it takes place: The priest first consecrates the Host, "This is My Body." Then he consecrates the wine, "This is My Blood." What takes place when blood is separated from the body? One DIES. Christ died once, and can die no more. The Mass is a re-enactment of that one Death, for your benefit and mine.

Now, for the "Love Station!" Just as Jesus gives Himself in love to the Father during the course of the Mass, I am invited to give myself to Jesus, so that when He gives Himself to the Father, the gift of me is included. Because I am given to the Father by His SON, the gift of myself takes on a greater quality. It is elevated to a divine level as Jesus, God's Divine Son, gives me to the Father. Now, here is the bonus for that gift of myself to Jesus. I receive within my soul, at the time of Communion, God Who IS Love. I am instantly upgraded, filled with love. The Mass is over and I, filled with love, go out into the world to share it with others. The week passes, and the hardships of the week always seem to slip me right back into myself and eventually I peter out with no more love to give. So the process of filling up at least once a week goes on continuously during life. How helpful to the soul if you can participate at Mass for a DAILY "fill-up." You are then able to dispense love continuously to those who don't have any. When you run out, you just go right back to Mass and get another "fill-up." You are then able to become a "love generator," something that the world needs more than anything else.

There are many of the faithful who are truly bothered about not being able to love one's enemies. You too may have a problem with that. The answer to that is not difficult. If you are filled with love, if you are "drunk" with love, whatever you do with whomever you have dealings, friend or foe, it's the same. Lovingly, you deal with your enemies because you do everything lovingly. Still another answer is this: your mind reminds you that everyone is a person. As you respect yourself as a person, you respect your enemy as a person. What he says, what he does, may grind you to pulp, but you love him for the fact that you are dealing with a "Who," not a "What."

Persecution of Christians is with us. It will become more intense as this century draws to a close. Suppose you were asked to give up your life for your faith — for Jesus. What do you think? You don't have to answer. Should Jesus ask this of you, He will see to it that you will be well prepared. Once in awhile give it thought. If you are to become a martyr in defense of your faith, all heaven will be at your side. What a glorious entry into heaven would be yours. Jesus speaks of this: "No one has greater love than this, to lay down one's life for one's friends." (John 15:13) If you live in your heart, there will not be a problem. If you are stuck in your head, hurry to get into your heart. It is where you need to be should you be asked to give up your life for what you believe.

There is an urgency today with regard to those who do not know Jesus, who are not aware of the basic essentials of life on this earth. To extend your love for God to those whom He loves is a necessary part of your friendship with Him. Our Lady asks for prayer, fasting, and evangelizing in favor of winning souls for Jesus. Tap into the resources that the Holy Spirit offers you in this area. When you feel a prompt or a nudge from Him, in favor of one soul or another, it's time to move and to move with confidence. He will tell you what to say and what to do.

To safeguard your love for God, yourself, and your neighbor, enter often into prayer. I encourage you strongly not just to say prayers but to pray from your heart. Enter deeply into your heart and allow yourself to be moved by the Holy Spirit to talk with Jesus, with the Father, with Mary your Mother, with your guardian angel, with the saints. Help is only as far away as a heart to heart contact with any member of the Trinity, with any of the saints and angels in heaven. I am not recommending that you pray much but to pray well. Pray always as a child would pray, with sincerity, with simplicity, with your whole being.

There is just one other matter that I should bring before your heart's eye. It is this. The ultimate expression of your love is to be of loving service to those in need. Here is the way Jesus puts it: "I was hungry and you gave me something to eat. I was thirsty and you gave me something to drink. I was a stranger and you welcomed me. I was naked and you gave me clothes. I was sick and you cared for me. I was in prison and you came to visit me." (Matt. 25:35-36) When you reach out to others less fortunate than you, and you do this because Jesus wants you to, merit is computed for you in heaven. Now, then, is the time for you to store up for yourself treasures in heaven. This is the bottom line of how a Christian is to imitate Jesus.

CHAPTER 12

Your Heart and
the Experience of Obedience

> *"He went down with them and came
> to Nazareth, and was obedient to
> them, and his mother kept all these
> things in her heart."*
>
> *(Luke 2:51)*

> *"And found human in appearance, he
> humbled himself, becoming obedient
> to death, even death on a cross."*
>
> *(Phil. 2:7-8)*

Obedience is the loving surrender of one's will to its God. It is when a human person, having been made in the image and likeness of God, makes use of the free will given to him/her by Him to fulfill the purpose for which one had been brought into existence. The person makes a choice to carry out whatever God is asking and had asked from the beginning of time. In addition to doing freely what God has ordained for each, the person has the inner power to say either yes or no to whatever it is that God wishes. Obedience is giving up one's will in favor of doing God's Will. To obey is to live in perfect harmony with the One Who is the Giver of life.

All of creation is brought into existence to give obedience to God. There is, however, a distinction to be made. Creatures are of two kinds: those endowed with a free will and those brought into existence to act, as God designed them to act, without the benefit of free will. Every creature reflects some attribute of God and is created to accomplish something specific within the entire framework of creation. In these creatures not having the power of choice, there is never a need to question at any moment what it is that they are to do. The most minute detail of their activities has been prearranged by the Divine Architect.

Human beings have been given the capability to do what God wishes of them and do it with complete freedom. In addition to being able to act freely, they can choose either to fulfill or not to fulfill their purpose for existence. All creation, other than those endowed with a free will, MUST do what they were created to do and MUST always act precisely according to a prearranged plan. They do not have the capability of deviating in the slightest from this plan. Humans, on the other hand, with the use of intelligence can reach out to search for God's Will. Making use of free will, they can follow through and act in accordance with the results of their findings.

One other factor distinguishes persons from all the other creatures. Human beings must take upon themselves responsibility for their behavior. Because they are capable of making choices, they will have to answer for the choices they make. If their choices are in favor of doing God's will, there is the promise of reward. If instead, their choices are in favor of doing their own will, a punishment can be expected. There is no reward or punishment meted out to the rest of creation. The rain will never be punished for causing a flood. The sun will never be rewarded for providing light and heat year in and year out. It is exciting and yet frightening to realize that human beings can either attain the eternal rewards of heaven or choose the everlasting fires of hell depending on the choices they make.

Obedience is a virtue. It is the most basic of virtues. It under-lies all of the others, and all of the others branch out from it. Even the virtue of charity, the most sublime of virtues, is prac-ticed because of an obedience to God's command to love. The final test in whether a person is genuine in the practice of virtue is whether he or she practices obedience. The Ten Commandments were given to be obeyed; the two great Commandments of love likewise are to be obeyed.

Jesus, as True God, was in no way bound to obedience. It was He Who was to be obeyed. Nonetheless, He came into the world to fulfill the wishes of His Father, to take our disobe-dience upon Himself, to give us a model of obedience, and to submit in total obedience to every wish of His Father, even that of undergoing death on the Cross.

Obedience offers the greatest antidote to pride. Observing it a soul is able to practice the virtue of humility. Lucifer's pride was what caused him to disobey God. Reflecting upon himself and observing his greatness, he chose not to surrender to the Will of God. His pride made him blind to his need for God. Pride and obedience do not mix. True humility invites genuine obedience. Where there is humility, obedience follows closely behind. Humility is a reminder to the human soul that it is totally dependent on God for every breath and for each heart-beat. Every creature on the face of the earth depends on God as its very source of life. Human beings who are capable of appreciating this total dependence can find it easier to bend to God's Will. When they come upon the realization that Jesus died for their sins to give them an opportunity to enter Heaven, their obedience is even practiced joyfully. To obey God is not a matter of charity. It is a matter of justice. God deserves to be obeyed in appreciation of the gift of life, the gift of redemption.

One can gain a deep respect for the virtue of obedience by giving thought to the great punishments inflicted on those of the human race who chose to be disobedient. Just imagine one having to remain in hell forever and ever as must Satan and those angels who went along with him in his disobedience. Imagine, too, how all human beings who die in serious rebellion must make their permanent home in hell. Consider the grave consequences of the act of disobedience on the part of Adam and Eve. Visualize, if you can, the number of souls who will receive the punishment of the eternal fires for having rejected the redemptive grace earned for them by Jesus. The thought of all this is sobering and makes obedience easier to take in contrast.

The many and fruitful benefits of obedience cannot be measured by any instrument. To have spent some years living in obedience and then to discover that a person can merit the eternal blessings of heaven, is in human terms a very good bargain. A countless number of our brothers and sisters in the human race won the greatest crowns of glory for their life of obedience. Saints like Our Blessed Mother, St. Francis of Assisi, Maximilian Kolbe, St. Maria Goretti, and millions of others have gone before us to give us the example of heroic obedience. You, too, can live in hope that by practicing this virtue you can merit a crown of splendor for yourself.

How many there are in our human family who were martyred for their obedience to God and paid the great price of their lives. In our own time, many thousands of Christians all over the world are being put to death for their obedience. It comes down to a battle between pride and humility, between obedience and disobedience. It is a battle that carries with it eternal consequences.

Obedience does not come naturally. It has to be practiced. In fact, it seems to go against the grain of our natural self. Once a person places himself/herself on a pedestal and manages to look down on others, obedience is set aside. When the love for money and power enter into the spiritual bloodstream of a person, the sense of dependency evaporates, pride sets in, and obedience is trampled on. The more egocentric the person, the greater the danger one has of losing God forever.

What a precious moment in your life when, with as much heart as you can come up with, you speak such words as, "I WANT to be obedient. I WANT to be humble." To voice these words is the very beginning of being able to live a life of obedience. Grace follows such a disposition and makes obedience a source of joy.

As you continue on your journey from the head to the heart, there is a big mountain to climb. One ultimately lives either by logic or obedience. Logic means doing what makes sense. Obedience is that which makes sense to God. The first is of the head, the second of the heart. If you really would like to take a shortcut on your journey, put great effort into attaining the experience of humility. If ever you would wish to get out of your head quickly and go directly and instantly into your heart, find something to do out of obedience. As soon as you put forth an act of obedience, you are already in your heart. The mind does not know how to obey. As the eye cannot hear, so the mind cannot obey.

Every act of obedience registers in heaven. It is a good idea to get serious about making obedience a greater priority. Here is a suggestion: Within the course of one day, keep track of the number of times you use the pronoun "I" in your speech. It may surprise you. It goes something like this: I have to get out of bed. I have to take a shower and brush my teeth. I have to get off to work. That is probably how your day starts. Now, instead of the word "I," substitute the words "Jesus wants me to." "Jesus wants me to get out of bed. Jesus wants me to take a shower. Jesus wants me to brush my teeth." If slowly you can get out of the habit of using the pronoun "I" and turn your words into "Jesus wants me to" you will change your life around. Instead of making yourself the center of your life, you will put Jesus into the center of it. Each time you say this with your heart, you are doing something in obedience to God. You might begin by prefacing this phrase to those things which you are already doing. Surely, it needs no stretch of the imagination to realize that God does want you to be neat, to be helpful, to give service. This very simple practice will change not only your life here on earth but also the quality of your life in heaven.

What would you say is the cause of all the evil in our world today, in fact, in the whole world in the past? Suppose everyone practiced obedience. It would be like heaven on earth. We will be coming into that kind of life that is being called the new era. It will be a life of obedience, a life of humility and, consequently, a life of peace and joy. Could it not be true that the more intellectual an age, the harder it is for that age to enter into obedience? It would seem so. We are such a "thinky" generation. There is a large segment of the population who would find it almost impossible to make a journey from the head to the heart. In fact, it is easier for most people to make the journey from the heart to the head. All of us were in the heart when we were little. It is an interesting fact that God so designed human nature as to start life in the heart. He made it so — with purpose — that the child does not attain the age of reason until about its seventh year. His plan is obvious. He started life for you on the foundation of goodness not smarts. Sad but true. Television has harmed and continues to do harm to little children. They are made to begin their active thinking prematurely, and this is in direct opposition to the way that God planned it.

Satan feeds on our generation. He has it within his power to tamper with your mind but he cannot touch you if you are in your heart, especially if you are spending time believing, trusting, loving, or obeying. You'll have to admit that in your own experience, most temptations begin in the head. There enters an unchaste thought, a jealous thought, a proud thought. That is only the beginning. Thoughts are connected with feelings and feelings, for most people, govern behavior. It has been proven in history that just as soon as an age becomes highly intellectual, pride comes in like a cancer. With pride floating around in the environment, it tends to become a breeding place for Satan. This is not a hypothesis. It's a fact.

Political correctness is what governs much of the world today. It is one of the cancers of our age. What the world promotes is that God and conscience have no part in modern society. What does this amount to? Obedience is out; what is of advantage to the person is in. The problem has its roots in the deification of the individual. It is what can be expected of a generation that has made the individual a god and has pushed aside the real God.

Our Church is in a crisis. It has been in crises before but I don't think any of those in the past have been as crucial as the one that is present in our day. Its very foundation is being rotted out from under it. That foundation is obedience. The Church's foundation is set upon the authority of the Vicar of Christ and the bending of faithful, both cleric and lay, to that authority. The enemy has tried for centuries to destroy the Church. First, through secular dictators who set themselves up against it and second, through the immorality that plagued it from the heights to the depths of its human element. The enemy had failed in the past. Now things are different because the enemy is within. The biggest gun being used is the internal gradual corrosion of obedience. There has entered into the Church in its human element a spiritual virus that has caused many to shift life from that which is based in the heart to that which is based in the head. It is as simple as that. Major surgery is the only hope. It is Jesus' Church. Jesus is God. The Holy Spirit is the Giver of Life within the Church. He is God. Our

Blessed Lady is the Mother of the Church. She is the Spouse of the Holy Spirit Who is God. St. Joseph is the protector of the Church. He is very close to God. Because God is still in charge, the enemy will be defeated. Obedience in the remnant is very much alive. God will use this faithful group, steadfast in obedience, to give new life to the Church. Obedience will never go out of style. As long as God exists, obedience is certain. God is eternal.

As a Christian, your lifeline is a life of obedience. It has been your training that God is obeyed through lawful authority. Lawful authority can be either of the State or of the Church. "Give to Caesar what belongs to Caesar, and to God what belongs to God." (Matt. 22:21) It is Christian to obey the lawful authority of the State. It is Christian to obey the lawful authority of the Church. There should be no conflict. The primary scope of responsibility belonging to the State is the physical welfare of its people. The primary scope of responsibility belonging to the Church is the spiritual welfare of the faithful. It is God's wish by His own design that there should be harmony between the body and the soul. It is His wish that there be harmony between the State and the Church. In this day of ours, we, as Christians, have serious problems. The lawful authority of our country is making something legal that according to God's law is sinful. It is your belief as a Christian that in issues pertaining to life within the State, you are not to obey a law if it is contrary to God's law. The Church has never made laws that are contrary to lawful government. The State under the legislative powers of the lawful appointed leaders, has on many occasions in history made laws that seriously oppose the laws of God. What then does all this mean for the Christian? He is simply to obey God rather than man. Penalties? Fines? Imprisonment? Death? Yes. Our heritage as Christians is one in which thousands upon thousands of the faithful have suffered much, even death, in remaining faithful to the laws of God. As it has happened in the past, and is happening in our own day, we know that the conflict is real and we may have to face it sooner than we think.

The real battle sifts down to the battle between those of the head and those of the heart. If you remain obedient to the lawful authority of the Church, you will be made to suffer. There is no love in Satan. Satan makes use of the State. By the amount of evil in which the world is submerged, it is clear that Satan is very much alive and doing exceedingly well in his own estimation. Satan is not of the heart. His angelic "heart" had turned to stone and is filled with hatred. His greatest hatred is being directed against His Maker. He knows that he cannot cause harm to God directly. He can, nonetheless, cause harm to His people. Satan is working in such a way as to eradicate the world of goodness and what that means ridding the Church and the world of obedience to God. He is gaining ground by making use of subtleties. He is watering down obedience through rationalization. He is gradually dissolving the activities of the heart by hyper-activating the minds of those whom he is in the process of enslaving to himself. It is his main thrust to rob human beings of their freedom to obey God by gradually enslaving them to himself. He is doing this through the hyper-stimulation of the minds of a large number of the members of the human race. This is not a suspicion. It is a fact that is well on its way to becoming universally accomplished.

What then is the way of action, of defense, of strategy for the Christian? It is that the Christian must become strengthened in the virtue of obedience. This strengthening is best through prayer and working with the Holy Spirit. In any event, your life in the future as a Christian will not be easy. Your own will oppress you and, in time, Satan's army will even turn itself on those of your own who earlier had oppressed you. He will use the enemy within the Church to confuse you, to make it difficult to be obedient, and then he will turn on those whom he used initially against the remnant, and put forth all of his powers to wipe Christ's Church off the face of the earth. He is attempting to do this with hopes that he will become the god of earth. He has waited centuries to accomplish this. It bears repeating that as the Pharisees sneered with glee when they saw Christ dead on the Cross, the enemy will do the same when it believes that it has destroyed the Church. As the Pharisees were stunned when Jesus came back to life, so its enemy will be stunned when the Church surges forth with greater life than ever.

For your own survival, get to know your enemy. Withdraw more and more from that part of worldly life that is already under Satan's domination. Continue to improve the quality of your prayer life. Keep in close touch with the Holy Spirit. He will fill your soul with wisdom, with clarity of thought, and with super courage. Keep your heart's eye on the glory God promises to those who remain faithful. Put your heart's eye also on the consequences of disobedience. Keep your Christian soul riveted to the reward of obedience and the horrible, horrible punishment of its contrary.

CHAPTER 13

Your Heart and the Experience of Forgiveness

> *"Then Peter approaching asked him, 'Lord, if my brother sins against me, how often must I forgive him? As many as seven times?' Jesus answered, 'I say to you, not seven times but seventy-seven times.'"*
>
> (Matt. 18:21-22)

Forgiveness is one of the most difficult qualities to find within one's soul. The reason for this is that there is no forgiveness in the mind and, in our day, most people spend most of their time using their minds. They have the thought of forgiveness; they believe that, that is what they are doing but they are not. Forgiveness is found only in the heart. As you cannot smell with your ears, so you cannot forgive except from the heart.

Forgiveness is a quality of the heart wherein a person, who has been harmed in some way, melts away the resentment that usually comes with the hurt and makes the one who has caused the hurt know honestly and sincerely, that he does not hold any ill feeling at what was said or done. The one hurt behaves toward the offender as if the offense never occurred. Obedience enters into forgiveness because the Master insists that His followers practice it. Charity enters into forgiveness because, as God has lovingly forgiven our sins, He wishes that His love is reflected in the forgiving of the hurts and/or sins directed against us.

As you, dear reader, recite the Lord's Prayer, you are constantly reminded of the fact that your sins are forgiven as you yourself forgive others. This sounds a warning from God, which Jesus Himself expresses in the parable of the servant who was first forgiven his debt by the master and then refused to forgive the debt of a fellow servant. On hearing of this, the master was very angry. You can understand, I am sure, that unless one abides within one's heart, it is impossible to find within one's self the power of obedience. If the heart is not at least activated by obedience, one cannot possibly elicit an act of forgiveness.

Due to the adverse mental climate of today, people are not forgiving because they are not able to. The inability to forgive causes one hurt to nurse another. The mind dwells on it and, with the hurt constantly bouncing around in the mind, feelings like anger, resentment, and revenge arise. These in themselves are a punishment for not forgiving. The more they are harbored, the greater is the crippling effect that takes hold of the soul. The person who has caused the hurt may have already confessed it, forgotten all about it, and gone merrily along in life. The person suffering the hurt because of his inability to forgive, continues to be wretched, miserable, and full of self-pity.

To have to work with one hurt is not that bad, but you know as well as I that one is highly blessed if one carries only a single hurt. Each one of us collects them on the way through life as barnacles latch onto the sides of a ship. The ordinary person who is unable to forgive faces and deals with a mountain of hurts, some bigger and more devastating than others. Ultimately, the hurts weigh one down until there comes a hurt that plunges a person over the edge. The hurting mind breaks apart, loses all enthusiasm for life and may end up in an institution for the mentally and emotionally ill. As a priest for many years, I have met these victims of enumerable unforgiven hurts. Psychiatric wards are filled with people who struggle through life dragging along these heavy balls and chains, unable to smile, unable even to eat, and unable to carry on a normal life.

Living the Gospels is the best answer. If one is a genuine Christian, making an effort to follow the directives and the commandments of Jesus, he/she can lead a peaceful life. Jesus points out, "The truth will make you free." (John 8:32) Of course, you realize that living the Gospel life is living the heart life. There can be no substitute. One can try to rationalize hurts or take medication to lessen their pain but, unless one's heart melts them down, they just will not dry up and blow away.

Not too long ago, I received a phone call from a lady under great distress because she was unable to forgive her husband for hurts that he had caused her. The marriage was on its last leg. She said, "I have prayed and prayed. I pleaded with God to help me to forgive him, but I CAN'T! I CAN'T!" My response, prompted by the Holy Spirit, I am sure, was this: "As much as you can from your heart, say this to Jesus. 'Jesus, if you want to forgive him, go ahead. You can forgive him through me.'" It worked. A few months later she phoned with gratitude that the marriage had been saved. As soon as she had given Jesus permission to forgive her husband, grace was given to her soul and the heavy burden was taken away. To my mind, it is a good solution. To fall is human, to forgive is divine. With help from above, the most severe hurts can be and are truly being healed. It is forgiveness that is the best and cheapest medicine for body and for soul.

How many times have you heard the statement, "I forgive you, but I will NEVER forget what you did."? That is not a true act of forgiveness. Just imagine if Jesus would say that to us after each confession. When He forgives, He forgives. The sins no longer exist. Nor does He ever bring them up again. This is what He expects of His followers — a clean break. There is something that can be mentioned here even though it might come up again later, and it is this: One must remember that each person is to be in charge of his or her mind. If one is in the heart, the heart has power and says to the mind, "I DON'T WANT you to think of that hurt again." If the person means business and the mind gets the message, such a power over the mind helps for peace of soul.

Living in a state of loving makes forgiveness a snap. Grace is needed. It comes as needed when the heart is receptive, soft, and warm. When there is a mellowness and a gentleness of spirit within a person, hurts are absorbed one by one and are not allowed to mount up. Aligning each hurt to the hurts of Jesus makes it bearable. Recycling each hurt by offering it for the poor souls in purgatory, or in atonement for one's own sins, causes the hurt to be productive spiritually for one's self and for others.

There is still another lesson that Jesus wishes to teach His followers. Yes, they are to forgive seventy times seven but, in addition to that, He asks of us that we be quick and ready to ask for forgiveness. It is music to the ears of a wife when her husband approaches her and says, "Honey, will you forgive

me?" It is the same inner experience of certain joy when she comes to him with the same question. Children approach their parents to ask for forgiveness and, likewise, there are times when, for the edification of the children, the parents can be
⁵ heard asking to be forgiven for some hurt they caused a child or the children. When that important question is directed sincerely and from the depths of one's heart, the response can be equally a source of elation and peace for both. "Of course, I forgive you," or "I am just so delighted to be able to forgive
¹⁰ you." There are times one would say to another, "Oh, I forgave you days ago even without your asking. Now that you have asked for forgiveness, I forgive you double." There is joy in the family, and a lot of healing takes place at a time when members ask each other for forgiveness. Imagine how much
¹⁵ additional joy is experienced in heaven when some poor soul who had strayed comes to Jesus' representative in the confessional to ask Him for forgiveness. It truly delights one's heart to believe that if one makes a request to be forgiven Jesus does really and truly forgive on the spot. There is no dillydallying.
²⁰ When true sorrow motivates a soul to ask Him for forgiveness, Jesus, with a joyous Heart, returns His response directly to the heart. "Of course, of course, of course." Here is how Jesus expresses it to His faithful listeners: "What is your opinion? If a man has a hundred sheep and one of them goes astray,
²⁵ will he not leave the ninety-nine in the hills and go in search of the stray, and if he finds it, amen, I say to you, he rejoices more over it than over the ninety-nine that did not stray." (Matt. 18:12-13)

As you very well know when you were inspired to forgive
³⁰ someone for something that they had done to hurt you, humility is required of you to forgive them from your heart. It takes equal humility, if not more, to ask for forgiveness. People who do not live in the heart cannot come forth with humility. There is much sadness in our world precisely on that account.
³⁵ People who have done some damage to relatives, friends, and others do not have the humility to ask to be forgiven.

You may also have heard the statement after someone has asked to be forgiven. "I don't know. If I forgive you, you will turn right around and hurt me again. What is the use of me forgiving you? I have forgiven you in the past and, look, you have hurt me again and now you expect to be forgiven just like that. I'm sorry, I have to think about it." They may be expressing a valid gripe, save for the words of Jesus quoted beneath the title of this chapter. One must be ready to forgive "seventy times seven." Moral theology teaches that in some cases, it is allowed for a short time to withhold forgiveness for a good reason but it should not be delayed for more than three days. Just consider the behavior of Jesus in this same situation. I go to confession with sorrow. I am forgiven. Three weeks later, I go to confession to confess that I had slipped into the same sin. Jesus forgives again, and again. To my mind, and know that I speak only for myself, it would do me some spiritual good if once in a while Jesus, speaking through the priest, would say something like, "I don't know about you. You have been confessing the same sin for three years. It would seem to me that by now you would have repented of it." He would be justified to say something like that but He does not. He leaves it up to me to resolve my repeated failures. There is never any harshness. if I confess to the same sin it may be that Jesus' words through the priest would come out in such a fashion that I would be encouraged to avoid the particular repeated sin and I would receive some counsel on how best this might be done.

There is one problem that never seems to go away when people continue to go to confession. It is one that does untold spiritual damage to the penitent. What is it? You may be surprised when you hear it. It is this. From my many years of transmitting God's forgiveness to the penitent, I have found that more than many penitents do not forgive THEMSELVES. I believe that this is one of the major causes of backsliding into having to ask pardon for the same sin time after time. It comes out in words something like this, "Watch, I'll do it again, just watch." These words are said even after repeating in the act of contrition, "I firmly resolve ... ." What surfaces here, once again, is the lack of discipline over the mind. Without a doubt Satan gets in on the taunting. He can and does work on the mind. As long as the tape of certain failure runs on and on in the mind, one almost talks oneself into falling again and again. There is something definitely just not right when a scenario such as this goes on. Turning to the Holy Spirit for help is the best solution. Being able to say, "Holy Spirit, I give up. I have tried to avoid this sin for years and still I fall. I can't do anymore. I've had it. Help me! Help me!" When such desperation comes from the depths of one's being, the Spirit is right there on the spot to offer help.

It is easy to become hardened to sin. It is also easy to become so proud that one would deny that there is such a thing as sin. Something has happened among the faithful of our day. I have personally seen the change. I used to hear confessions for hours. There were lines and lines of penitents. Now, very few people admit needing to confess. Why? Faith has been weakened and, with the weakening of faith, reverence has lessened. With the lessening of reverence, rationalizing with regards to one's behavior has taken over. Again and again the mind does the heart damage. Nothing will change unless and until some calamity befalls the human race to get it back onto its knees. God loves His people enough that, if it is a calamity they need to become humble, I believe that He will oblige.

It might not be a bad idea for you, dear heart, to put your book down for a few minutes in order to munch on this important topic of forgiveness. Loss of heaven can be at stake. The need for true sorrow to be generated within the soul is a must for all of us. God's mercy is everlasting, but even He knows how to say, "Enough is enough!"

CHAPTER 14

Your Heart and the Experience of Gratitude

> *"Jesus said in reply, 'Ten were cleansed, were they not? Where are the other nine? Has none but this foreigner returned to give thanks to God?'"*
>
> *(Luke 17:17, 18)*

*G*ratitude is a virtue that is very dear to God. It is a quality that all parents would like to see in their children. It is something beautiful to behold in any person. Surely, it is a delight when we find it within ourselves.

As you can very well gather by now, there is no gratitude in the head. Any smallest bit of gratitude that anyone has must come from the heart. There is no other source. People can say they are grateful but, if they are only thinking it, it is found only on their lips. In our day, with television as a teacher, the multitudes have become good actors. One can act out gratitude. If gratitude is not experienced within the heart, it is not gratitude at all. Here, of course, we must be careful. No one really knows what goes on within the spirit of anyone unless it is revealed by the person. If someone states that he or she is grateful, it does not behoove anyone to be judgmental. It is proper to take one's word if claim is made that one voices gratitude sincerely. Nonetheless, for you who are so willing to find a more perfect life and model yourself on the life of Jesus, do know that your heart must be engaged if there is to be genuine gratitude found in your soul.

Our first training in gratitude comes from our parents when we are very small. When your Auntie gave you a lollipop, mother was quick to coach you, "What do you say to Auntie?" You knew what to say and you said it because it was what you were supposed to do. Maybe by the time you were in high school and someone gave you a ride home because you missed the late school bus, you remembered that you should be grateful. By that time, without a doubt, your gratitude was real. Gratitude has to be practiced. It is not part of our fallen nature. The most important statement made thus far is this one: Unless you are able to express a hearty gratitude to people whom you can see and hear, it is not easy at all to extend gratitude to God Whom you cannot see or hear.

Hopefully, there has come a time in your life when your mind has reported to you through grace, that God has been good to you. Most of the time this comes later in life when we have been tried and tested. Here, with all of the other virtues that you are invited to practice, the mind can be helpful if we ask it to be. If you were to sit yourself down and say to your mind with a degree of authority, "Mind! I want you to bring up before me all of the blessings that I have received from God." It may balk a bit. If it does, go back a little and demand that it brings up from its memory some good things that people have done for you. Note, before it will do even this for you, you yourself must be quiet within your spirit and be genuinely interested. One should never play games with the mind. Doing so will teach it not to take you seriously. Gratitude, in its very best expression, is directed to God the Giver of all good things. Grace makes it possible for you to do this. You already know that the Holy Spirit is the Giver of life. He is also the Giver of all good things. Of course, Jesus gives and the Father as well. Mother Mary is an Obtainer of good things for Her children. She must, however, go through any of the Members of the Trinity as a Daughter, as a Mother, as a Spouse. The angels and saints, too, are able to intercede for you for the things you need. Ultimately, it is the Holy Spirit Who will prompt you to go to the one or the other. As He directed Jesus' Life in all of its details while on earth, He will do the same for you. God is extremely generous! If you would sit yourself down and begin to ponder with the help of the Holy Spirit on how His generosity has touched you, it would take you a good week. You would begin with the fact that He even thought of you. When He thought of you, He created an image of you for Himself and then decided to create you. Throughout your life so far, He has supplied your every need. I don't say want because He works with needs first. If your wants are something that will bring Him greater glory and assist you to grow in virtue, surely He also responds to wants such as these. His generosity is primarily extended in the direction of getting you into heaven where He will have you with Him for all eternity. In addition, He will want you with Him so that He can enjoy your company and, gaze upon you with joy for all eternity because you chose Him and made Him first in your life. What a surge of gratitude would come from your heart were you to come to an understanding of how special He has made you to Himself.

5   Going beyond the blessings that He has given to you personally, there are so many more that He has given to you through others. For instance, your parents and, before them, their parents, who made it possible for you to have the mother and father whom God formed for you as gifts. Brothers and sisters
10   are gifts as well. Surely relatives and friends are likewise gifts from God, not to say anything about enemies. Enemies serve as a source of a blessing or two, especially that of growing in patience and humility. The universe is yours to accept as a gift from Him for your personal enjoyment, by way of its beauty
15   and its usefulness. God's generosity to you is without measure. If daily you would allow yourself to be reminded of the blessings that God continually bestows on you, you would walk, talk, and even breathe submerged in the heart quality of gratitude. Your happiness on this side of death will be greatly
20   enhanced as the virtue of gratitude instills itself within you.

Let me offer you a particular message given by Jesus to see what you think about it. It is: "To the one who has, more will be given; from the one who has not, even what he has will be taken away." (Mark 4:25) Read it over once again. What do
25   you think of it? Does it not seem very unfair? It would seem to me that God in His goodness would be more moved to give to those who have less or nothing but here is Jesus saying that those who HAVE are the ones who will receive more. You won't have to think much more about it, if you put into the
30   equation the notion of gratitude. Whoever has AND IS GRATEFUL, will receive more. Same with the second segment: Those who have not, and are UNGRATEFUL, and so on. Is this not true even for you as you give to others? If they are grateful for what you give them, you don't mind giving
35   them more. If, on the other hand, they are not grateful, you look to someone else for your giving. Parents are the same

way with their children. Those who are grateful for what they receive are much more generously treated.

The degree of your humility will have a major part to play in the quality of your gratitude. Humility recognizes the fact that all that you have is from God. You are not your own. You belong to Him. You owe your life to Him and everything good that comes with it.

Once again, it would be helpful in your journey if you would tarry momentarily before reading on. Question yourself concerning the quality of your own gratefulness, especially to God but also to others around you. Remember the short cut. It's the Holy Spirit!

CHAPTER 15

Your Heart and the Experience of Reverence

"Then he taught them saying, 'Is it not written: "My house shall be called a house of prayer for all peoples?" But you have made it a den of thieves.'"

(Mark.11:17)

One of the most distinctive qualities of the Christian is his/her display of reverence. Jesus is the model of reverence. He is God, and yet the reverence He directed toward His Father, His Mother, and all human beings, as well as for all creatures of nature, is altogether remarkable. 5
Reverence is a heartfelt recognition of the sacred. Sacredness is the quality or condition of the divine attribute — holiness — in a person, place or thing. God is the central focus of reverence. When this reverence is expressed directly to Him, it is known as adoration. When reverence is expressed 10 indirectly to God, it is directed to sacred persons, places or things which are identified with God.

Reverence is not found in people who are without faith. Belief is the chief support of reverence. Reverence is profound within an individual when faith is alive. Where faith is weak, 15 so is reverence. What is the inner connection between the two? First of all, both reside within the heart. Reverence is a satellite of faith. It rides with it. What lessens the reverence within a soul? The lessening of faith. What increases the reverence within a soul? An increase in faith. What brings on an 20 increase of faith? Prayer. What is prayer? A conversation with God. All of these, as you can see, are interrelated.

Prayer before the Blessed Sacrament is very powerful. Jesus speaks of Himself as the Living Bread. Bread is the staff of life to the body. Living Bread is the Staff of Life to the soul. You 25 have seen people who have more life in them than others. No one usually gives it much thought as to why. Why is it that some people are so vibrant and others are so listless? Medical people will come up with all kinds of answers and perhaps in many cases they are right. But much of a person's level of life 30 comes from the soul. As it gives support to the body, an enlivened soul also gives the body more energy, and — this should not be surprising — better health. Jesus IS Life. It stands to reason that if a person taps into His Life, he/she will have more life. Belief in Him makes it possible for the Life of 35 Jesus to be lived in the soul of one in His presence. It is here, praying before Jesus in the Blessed Sacrament, that the soul is able to enhance itself in faith and at the same time, deepen its reverence.

5 A Catholic Church is THE HOUSE OF GOD. This is so because of Jesus' presence within it. There are other churches in some limited way dedicated to God, but it is not the same because Jesus is not there in a Sacramental presence. But, you say, Jesus Himself said, "For where two or three are gathered together in my name, there am I in the midst of them." (Matt.
10 18:20) What Jesus says here obviously is true. A non-Catholic church is but a building. People do not have to gather in a building for Jesus to be in their midst. There is a difference in what kind of presence Jesus speaks. There is a "spirit" presence and a "physical" presence. In the latter, Jesus speaks of
15 His Flesh and His Blood as something very physical and very spiritual: "Jesus said to them, 'I tell you the truth, unless you eat the flesh of the Son of Man and drink His blood, you have no life in you.'" (John 6:53) There is definitely a physical presence of Jesus in the Eucharist as He RESIDES in the
20 Tabernacle.

Can you picture yourself living centuries ago, when Jesus walked this earth and being in His physical presence? You would have been able to see Him, hear Him, touch Him. This is the same Jesus Who resides within the Catholic Church.
25 When you enter, you may very well say, " Good day, Jesus. I have come to be with you for a few minutes." Yes, it is the Consecrated Host, but it's JESUS! He is alive. He is real. He IS there as the Person of the God Man. When you are within His Home, you can feel comfortable in conversing with Him
30 as you would with any person whom you visit within his or her home.

To a mind not submerged in faith, the above does not make sense. It is all a matter of the imagination. When the human heart beats with the gift of faith, the mind still does not under-
35 stand, but it says OK. It reasons, "If Jesus said it, then it must be true even if I don't understand how it could be."

How the faithful behave when they are in Church will give you a reading as to how deep is their belief. If their manner is casual and they carry on as if they were out in the parking lot, then there is serious trouble. The body and soul are united in this earthly life. The body reflects what goes on in the soul. If the body does not present a reverential posture, then the soul is not "pumping" reverence into it. The belief meter is almost on "E.". That spells danger. When a soul is running out of belief it must make an effort to go for a "fill up." It is a bit ironic. Here the people are at the "belief station" in front of the Tabernacle that houses Jesus' Real Presence, and they do not make the effort to increase their faith. This is why I had said to you that if you wish to increase your reverence, pray to Jesus in front of the Tabernacle.

The Church building has been consecrated. That means it has been made sacred. It has been taken out of the realm of being something simply of the world; it has been designated as a place that belongs to God. It deserves respect. The demeanor of the people should reflect this respect. Respect should be displayed both in soul and in body. Once through the doors of the church, as God's House, a different disposition, one that is reverent, should become manifest. External behavior exhibits internal disposition: As God's House, it is a place of prayer not just a place to say prayers. Deference should be given to others so that the individual in no way interferes in or distracts from the prayer life of the rest. Noise is not conducive to prayer. The psalmist puts it this way: "Be still, and know that I am God. I will be exalted among the nations, I will be exalted in the earth." (Ps. 46:10) There is an order for silence in museums, hospitals, and theaters. These are of the world. Should not this be a trademark of God's House? Of course it should.

In addition to places which have been consecrated to God, there are persons who are set apart by a special consecration which makes them worthy of reverence. All persons, having been created in the image and likeness of God, deserve to be revered. In addition, there are those whom God has selected to carry on His work among His people. The first among these is the priest. He is special to God. He has the responsibility of administering to God's people by giving them the services that are required to assist them in the salvation of their souls. It is vital for each one of us once again to make the distinction between the WHO and the WHAT. The priest remains human even if he carries out divine functions. He entered the priest-hood as a human with talents and limitations. These remain throughout his priesthood. It is the WHO in him that deserves reverence. If his talents surface as he gives his service, God be praised for that. If his limitations come to the foreground, then God be merciful.

Should the priest be failing the people under his care, he is in need of prayer. If the priest is leading the faithful astray, and/or is giving public scandal, such a situation should be made known to the bishop. If it is a bishop who is failing as a true shepherd of his flock, charity must still prevail and prayer will be helpful. If, however, the shepherd is leading the flock away from the teachings of the Church, He gives up his right to be obeyed by the faithful. As times within the Church become even more confusing and less reverent, one is to follow one's conscience and put one's self under the direction of the Holy Spirit. To look for guidance and assistance from faithful priests, or faithful laity, would also be suggested.

In addition to priests, there are others consecrated to God. They are known as religious, as Sisters and Brothers. They have been selected by God in order to lead a vowed life of virtue and loving service. For this they are deserving of rever-ence. Should any one of these fail God, the mandate of charity would require the faithful to pray for them and to assist them in whatever way might be possible.

May I mention again the need of reverence to every single human being simply because they are reflections of God's love. Each one has been put into our midst by His creative power. It is a Christian's responsibility to give reverence to every person regardless of what their personal qualities might be. This reverence is due to every person simply because he or she is made in the image and likeness of God.

Finally, there are things which have been set apart from worldly use and designated in some way as sacred. These, too, are to be treated with reverence. These are known as sacramentals. They do not have the great power of the Sacraments but nonetheless, they are aids to us on our pilgrimage of faith. These are: Holy images, pictures, candles, palms, rosaries, medals, holy water, crucifixes, scapulars, and the like. They are not to be used in a superstitious manner. These objects have no power within themselves. They are to be used with reverence because through them is transmitted some spiritual help designated by the powers of the Church. It is the priest or deacon who is the ordinary minister of blessing such articles.

The responsibility to maintain one's self in reverence is a personal one. Help of all kinds is available, but prayer is the best — true prayer, prayer from the heart. The Holy Spirit is always available. If you really want to make ground in virtue and especially to become more reverent, it is necessary to have guard over your eyes, ears, and mouth. These need to be governed together by the head and the heart. If the head reports to you that you are, for example, thinking ill of someone, — thus the mind in its role of conscience — your will must come to the assistance of conscience and put power into ridding yourself of the thought. Humility is a great boost to reverence. When I know who I really am and what it is that I am on this earth to accomplish, it will be much easier for me to find reverence within my heart. Recalling your own failures and sins should help you to be more respectful of those who themselves are failing or have fallen into sin.

In closing, let it not be passed over or forgotten that you deserve to give yourself reverence. You are a person. That says a lot. Respect your mind for what it is because it helps to lead you to truth. Do not do anything to lessen its power, its clarity,

its usefulness. Your body, too, merits reverence. It is the temple of the Holy Spirit. It has been given to you to help you attain your goal in life. It should not be abused. Caring for it when it needs care is imperative. It should be respected since it chan-
5 nels the heart experiences and brings them to fruition.

Well, you've gone through material that is quite heavy. The considerations given might be somewhat tiring. Why not give yourself a treat for getting as far as you have on your journey. I would suggest that you give to yourself or do something for
10 yourself that you have never given or done in your entire life. Allow yourself to be creative in your choice.

CHAPTER 16

Your Heart and the Experience of Adoration

"And on entering the house they saw the child with Mary his mother. They prostrated themselves and did him homage."

(Matt. 2:11)

*A*doration is an expression of the heart which recognizes that God is the source of all creation, and of all good. It can be expressed only by a person, a creature endowed with free will. Animals are not capable of adoration. This, on the terrestrial level, belongs only to human beings. Angels are persons also endowed with a free will. Theirs is of a higher perfection. Their expression of adoration is purely spiritual and, so, more profound. Angels among themselves have each a distinct degree of adoration. Humans, while living in the body, have a characteristic form of adoration wherein the body and the soul are each postured in a way that is unique to each according to the specific qualities given to the body and those given to the soul. While the adoring posture of the body is largely dependent upon the soul, the soul can express an act of internal adoration somewhat independent of the body.

A prayer attributed to St. Augustine states: "You have created my heart for Thee, O Lord. It will not rest until it rests in Thee." What this means is that on creating human beings with a body and soul, the body has its five senses, i.e. smell, touch, taste, sight, and sound; the soul has its two faculties, i.e. the mind and the will or, the head and the heart. God put a particular feature into the heart similar to a compass always pointing to the north. The human heart, whether the mind is aware of it or not, points in God's direction. It was made to love Him and to be loved by Him. With man's free will, he can tamper with that direction. However, as much as he tries, he never finds happiness when he points that heart toward anyone or anything other than God. In creating man with a free will, God will never apply force to make him act according to that built-in direction. He can entice. He can coach. He can invite. He can do anything short of force to attract man's atten-tion. (I am using the word man in its generic sense — human — not as the person of masculine gender. In Latin, the first is translated into "homo," the second into "vir." English falls short in not making this distinction.) If the human heart latches on to anything or anyone other than God, the heart becomes dissatisfied, since that is not what it is to be after. The human heart then goes on searching. The heart does find joy in expressing love to a human being. It also finds a degree of fulfillment in this love. However all loving of the heart that is not connected with the love of God, satisfies for a time only. Its love of human being is deeper and more lasting as it is expressed within its love for God. The human heart was made to adore God. If it chooses to adore itself, another person, or anything else, by its very nature, it will find no lasting satisfaction. It is unhappy until it finds the One for Whom it was created, and does exactly what it was created to do. If a tiger, caged in a zoo just to be on exhibition, could speak, it would blast out that it is wretched because it did not come into life to be caged. It was made to to roam around in its own habitat, scot-free to do whatever tigers do. The human heart puts itself into bondage — into a cage — when it loves simply on the human level without the Divine Love pouring itself into it. The human heart is of such a nature that it is to love God with its whole being and love others only out of love for Him.

The first Commandment of God reads, "I am the Lord your God. You shall not put strange gods before me." God is a jealous God, not by fault, but by justice. He has a right to be adored by every person created by Him. He owns the universe. He owns all of the planets and stars and all that is in space. He owns every single creature created from the very beginning of time and all those He still plans to create. What does that mean for you and for me? It means that we do not belong to ourselves. We are His! He has given us life. He has given us freedom to choose Him or not to choose Him. This is one umbilical cord that may never be cut. God did not choose to give us life and then to spin us off into the world to be on our own. This is the mistake billions of people are making. They think that when they speak of independence, it means that one can do as one darn well pleases. That was never in God's Mind when He decided to create beings endowed with a will that is free.

I don't think that if you put one million airplanes into the sky dragging a huge sign behind them saying something like, "God made you, you know. You belong to Him!" that it would get much of a response. If some kind soul with a million dollars, wanting to do something special for God, would put the same message on CNN International, who would give heed to it? God has tried everything possible to get man's attention. With the fogged-up minds and hardened hearts of men refusing to give attention to God, He has almost given up. Do understand that He IS the Hound of Heaven. He will never give up on an individual of goodwill who is sincerely searching for Him. He speaks of the one sheep that has strayed, and what joy there is in heaven when one who has wandered off returns to Him. He has spoken of the prodigal son who went on his own. When, after all else failed to satisfy him in life, he returned home and was met not only with open arms but with a gala celebration as well.

It never ceases to be a source of amazement that with all the billions and billions of people in the world, how few are found to give adoration to the one true God. The Chosen People had an enormous problem with idolatry. They fell into it, were repentant for a time and then fell into it again. With so many, the first Commandment is ignored. These Commandments have been brought down to the two Great Commandments of love, and yet, there are so many who allow their hearts to go out to anyone or anything, but not to the true God. God has substituted the "Thou shalt nots ..." with the positive quality of love in "Thou shalt love the Lord your God with your whole heart ..." and it has made very little difference in mankind's attitude toward Him.

What I am going to say to you now is not an easy matter to digest. It is that the fallen Lucifer wanted to unseat God after he was created to be one of the most perfect angels. He was driven out of God's presence and is now roaming about seeking to become the god of earth. He has been seeking this glory from the time of Adam and Eve. He is working at it harder than ever in our time. I am not saying this with tongue in cheek. It is a fact! The reason he has gained so much is that he has convinced even those in high places that he does not exist. In this age of ours in which science dominates, multitudes conclude that if you can't see it, taste it, touch it, or smell it, hear it, it does not exist. Though scientists have done much to make life easier and more pleasant, they have also sold us short. The reason for this is that there is a spiritual dimension that cannot be measured by capturing a specimen in a test tube. Satan has taken an advantage and has been raking people over the and no one seems to blink an eye. I purposely bring him into this subject of adoration because he has been competing with God and is snatching souls from Him left and right. Why does not God annihilate him? It would be contrary to His nature to do that. He counteracts Satan's activities by giving sufficient grace to resist Satan to anyone who requests it.

In what area do you think that Satan is operating ? How is it that he is able to trick so many of God's children so painlessly and so cleverly? Remember, as a fallen angel, he has not lost any of his powers. He is brilliant, powerful, and cunning. Humankind has graduated from worshiping golden calves. With its upgraded intelligence, such an action is beneath its dignity. In what way is Satan wresting adoration from God to himself? In a way that has become highly refined and diabolically engineered.

The population of the modern twentieth-century is bent on having fun. It looks high and low to have a good time. Nothing is wrong with that. Up to a point. But what if almost everyone has gone beyond that point? To adore God means that He is to be first in the life of every man, woman, and child. He is to receive recognition as the source of all good from individuals, from companies, from religious groups, from governments, from every nation under the sun. Is He? Obviously not. He has been blotted out by constitutions, by laws, by dictators, by the United Nations. An attempt is being made for Him to be

removed from schools, from hospitals, from places of entertainment, from the media, from the armed forces, from all of
the humanistic religions, and from businesses. The time is at
hand when the enemies of God, sworn to create a society
completely detached from Him, are working feverishly to
abolish Him from the face of the earth. Those few, who are still
making use of conscience and free will to give Him the honor
He deserves, are becoming enemies of the state to be snuffed
out by force if necessary. Humanly speaking, it does not look
good for God. Let it be remembered — it is something very
easy to forget — God had met opposition before. He has
avenged Himself in history He will avenge Himself again. He is
showering His mercy upon humankind, but the time is at hand
when He will mete out justice for the fact that there is very
little response to that mercy.

Satan has the throngs "eating from his hands" and they
don't even know it. For anyone on the sidelines, it is as clear
as crystal. Adoration means putting God first in our lives. If so
many are not giving adoration to God, then to what and/or to
whom is adoration being given? What is it that holds a grip on
present-day humankind? It is legion: it is news worship,
money worship, fun worship, body worship, power worship,
self-worship. These and others all fall neatly into the category
of false worship. There are the sports idols, the Hollywood
idols, the news idols, the power idols, the rock idols, the guru
idols, the rich and famous idols, the gangster idols, the terrorist
idols, the jokester idols, the plastic card idols, the computer
idols, the stock idols, the political idols, the fair sex idols, the
muscle idols, the drug idols, the fast set idols, to mention
some. Every one of these takes away something that belongs
to God.

Who then can be saved? Our society is concretized into
many molds. Human beings have become like robots or like
pinballs in a pinball machine reacting to worldly stimuli
without thought of God or the consequences of their actions.
Men, women, and children are chasing after the pot of gold at

the end of the rainbow. Lottery tickets by the zillions go through the hands of billions seeking instant happiness. People live their lives placing money — its attainment, its use to gain power or influence — in first place as their most important god. But the Lord plainly said: "You cannot serve two masters; you cannot serve God and money." If money has become the super god under all of the other little god's mentioned above, then we must be assured that God will overcome money. He has overcome death. To overcome money will be, for Him, no difficult task.

God could get every single person on his/her knees if he wanted to use fear to win His people to Himself. All He would have to do is to speed up the rotation of the earth, from twelve hours, to six hours, to three hours, to one hour, until He would have all of the hardened hearts screaming for their lives. All He would have to do is to pull the one electric plug that runs the entire world. He could do it. There are a hundred and more ways that God could get humankind to its knees. He refuses to win His people over by any other way but love.

After all this by way of introduction, the question you might have already asked yourself is, "Is God first to me?" Who is more important to you, God or you? Do you spend more time with Him or with yourself? "Father," you say, "that's not fair." Perhaps not. I would not think of putting a guilt trip on you. There is a difference between judging, condemning, and making an effort to bring your relatives and friends to their senses. If you perceived that your mother or your brother were in serious danger, would you not do anything and everything within your power to save them? You would. God is a loving Father. Jesus is a caring Brother. The Holy Spirit is the Healer and Energizer. Mary is a concerned Mother. The saints in heaven are not sleeping. Be assured that they are actively working to snatch their relatives and friends away from the clutches of the serpent. The Holy Spirit is the first One to reach out to. Find Him. He dwells within you.

He is a Person. Give Him a person to person call. He will respond. It is His specialty to woo good-willed people away from the snares, away from trickery, away from the traps. Hopefully, you have traveled enough on the journey to know that the shortest cut into your heart is one little act of humility, one little act of obedience. Prayer from the heart, an honest down-to-earth conversation with Jesus before the Blessed Sacrament does wonders to keep your heart in humble adoration. There is time to work at putting God first. By the end of your journey from the head to the heart, it will become a reality. I assure you.

It has been a difficult subject. Take some time out. Give your steering wheel over to your Life Support System. They are a Team quite knowledgeable, quite capable, and quite eager to be at your side, to do for you whatever is necessary. Let Them.

CHAPTER 17

Your Heart and
the Experience of Discipline

*"Enter through the narrow gate, for
the gate is wide and the road broad
that leads to destruction, and those
who enter through it are many. How
narrow the gate and constricted the
road that leads to life. And those who
find it are few."*

(Matt. 7:13-14)

Discipline? Oh no! I could almost hear you say just that. It is not a pleasant or acceptable word in our time. Yet, of all the possible experiences of the heart, I would vote for this one to be at the top of the list. In my many years as a priest giving advice to people, this is the advice that I have had to give most frequently.

Discipline is a friend. It is not an enemy as many would want to believe. Once I have completed sharing with you what the Holy Spirit gives to me on the subject, you will be at peace when you learn that it will be of great support to you, not only on your journey from the head to the heart but on your entire journey through life from this moment to the moment when Jesus calls you home.

Here is one clear evidence that the head has its unique importance. You will have to depend on your head to learn more about yourself. Through your eyes and through your ears you will receive inklings of your own limitations, failures, sins. I point out to you the negative side because this is what discipline does best. It will come to your side to help you to shape up and fly right as you make efforts to go through the narrow gate Jesus speaks of. When your mind points out a flaw in your spiritual structure, the heart, prompted by the Holy Spirit will send you discipline to help put your house in order. There is usually not a very happy feeling when we see the house we live in and know that sooner or later we will have to clean things up. But I tell you one thing, when the mess is all cleaned up, there is an exhilaration that you cannot even begin to imagine.

No action will begin in the heart in putting discipline at your disposal, until you give the order for the heart to do it. This, too, is governed by the Holy Spirit if you have allowed Him space to do so. It always goes easier when He takes charge. Until you travel enough on your private journey from the head to the heart, you may not have enough natural strength to take charge of yourself. You may remember a few pages back, you learned about the gift of self to Jesus during the Mass. If there is no cohesive self, if you find yourself to be a bundle of habits and reactions, if you have not yet found your true self, you will not be able to make that gift of self. The Holy Spirit is the One Who takes charge if you are of good will. He does take the initiative in matters in which we are weak.

When I relate to you the need to take charge, I am making reference to you as a person. It is as a person that you are to say to your will, "I need your help. I need to be disciplined and I cannot do it without you." In this fashion you make friends with your will, give it the respect that it deserves, and work along with it.

In order to muster strength in your natural will which may be still expressing the weakness caused by Original Sin, it is a must that you train it. Just under ordinary circumstances of life in our day, it needs to be trained. If it is still in somewhat of a weakened state, grace cannot do much with it. Grace builds on nature. It is like a famous pianist. Let's say that he comes to visit you because he is a friend of one of your friends. He looks to see if you have a piano, and lo and behold he finds one. He sits down to begin one of his specialty pieces and wham— it sounds terrible. Your piano is very much out of tune. He is a professional pianist but when he tries to play on a defective piano his professionalism does him no good. It is the very same with the Holy Spirit. He is just great! He is able to do more for you than anyone else in the world. However, if your will is not up to snuff, He is very limited in what He can do.

There is a prescription that I would like to offer you to give your will an instant boost. Here it is: Give yourself five very easy orders during the course of the day for, let's say a week. Give these orders one at a time and do not give yourself the second order until you have obeyed the first. I repeat, easy orders. Let's say that your name is Tom or Tometta. You say to yourself by using your name, "Tometta, I want you to raise your right hand toward the sky." Do not obey automatically. It is vital that you experience within your heart the power to do just what you ordered yourself to do. Become well aware of what

the internal experience of obedience is like. It has a very distinct flavor. Here is an example of another order, "Tom, I want you to stamp your left foot." Again, make sure you do not do it automatically. You must follow through and learn the
5   experience of OBEYING YOUR OWN ORDER. After you have gone through the basics, you will become efficient in giving yourself all kinds of orders. What elation will be yours when you find out that the will obeys you. Now that I have given you this directive, and it has lodged itself into your head, it will not
10   do you a bit of good until you put it into practice. Just for a dry run: Give yourself the order to put this book down for the count of ten. Again don't do it as soon as you think of it, do it only when your will is engaged in an act of obedience. Go ahead, dare to do it, right now. One, two, three, four, five, six,
15   seven, eight, nine, ten. Hurrah! Silly? Not by a long shot. You will find it an opening to a higher level of life. Please, for your own welfare, don't let yourself off too easily on this prescription. Much depends on your following through.

Your will, now strengthened, becomes a great asset to you
20   in your spiritual life as well as in your ordinary everyday life. What is most hopeful is that the Holy Spirit will guide you in the building up of your natural will. He knows full well that as your natural will is strengthened, He will be able to do much, much more for you, with you, and through you. I am counting
25   on you to have enough love for yourself to take this seriously. Do not procrastinate. Get to it. Make it exciting for yourself as to what easy order you give to yourself. The aim is for you to become the captain of your own ship and ultimately to bring it to port.
30   The first task that you will be able to carry out with a will that obeys you will be to take charge of your mind. In ordinary life, all sorts of thoughts find their way into it. Whatever your five senses pick up, end up in your mind. This creates the problem of having all sorts of thoughts that do you no good
35   and take the space that prevent you from having higher quality thoughts. Remember this one liner: "I am not my mind, I have

a mind." People often become troubled over their thoughts. If they realized that their thoughts are separate from their person, they would be more at peace. For yourself, as a rule of thumb, you should only allow the thoughts that you want there. It is you who are to be in charge of your mind. You are to stand, so to speak, at the gate of your mind to check what it is that is trying to make its entry. If it is worthwhile, let it in; and if it is not worthwhile, with the help of your training, you will have the power to dismiss it. This will help you especially with impure and uncharitable thoughts. When your mind recognizes that you are its boss, it will listen to you and your life will become more peaceful.

To take another step, let's say that there is a person who has done you some harm. Every time you think of that person your feelings are aroused. When your feelings are aroused your level of productivity lessens. Your absorptive powers lessen. Your thinking loses sharpness. Now, when the thought of that person comes up, you can say to that thought, "Out! OUT!" It will obey, and you will spare yourself a lot of grief.

Your ability to make your mind obey you will also be of super help with impure thoughts. I am sure that you know of the chain that is connected to one of these. It goes from unexpected thought, to an impure feeling, to the arousing of the passion, and could easily lead you into sin. If you learn how to get rid of the thought by your command, your life will be more pure and you will become more stable. It will be the same with all your thoughts especially judgmental, uncharitable, and critical thoughts. These do great damage to one's spiritual life, to one's emotional life and to one's everyday practical life. Make another resolution now, while you are thinking about it, to strengthen your will. Do it with patience, but with firmness and constancy. Remember, only EASY orders from the start.

What can be accomplished with thoughts through discipline can also be done with emotions. Feelings make up a great part of life. Undisciplined thoughts and feelings have caused some to unravel to the point that institutional living is

the result. You have seen the behavior of a wild horse that needs taming. How is it done? The rider stays with the horse, allowing it to go through its tantrums until it has to yield to the strength of the trainer and breaks down. The wild horse is now
5   tamed. The same process must be gone through to bring raging feelings under control. Grace working through a strengthened will does wonders. Eruption of feelings can be lessened and conquered by first taking hold of the thought. That would be a shortcut. Another shortcut to the handling of
10 feelings is to prevent oxygen from getting to the thought. What that means is that the more attention paid to the thought, the longer it stays. It resists leaving. If the thought is ignored and replaced by another thought, feelings are held in abeyance. If the thought prevails and slips into the emotional department,
15 the task becomes more difficult.

It seems to be that impatience is about the most prominent of feelings to tame. Life on this planet is so fast, so demanding, and so complicated that impatience could begin to cling to the soul like a fungus. Family situations, especially when children
20 are around, and driving conditions on the busy highways, are two conditions of life which can cause ulcers, migraines, and depression. Every act of impatience brings about physiological harm. Becoming anxious about impatience just makes matters worse. At the root of impatience is the need to have
25 everything go one's own way. Bear in mind that only God has that right. Since I am not God, why should I think that everyone should do what I want them to or that everything should go as I think that it should. That is making your ego the center of all that happens around you. Impatience very easily brings on
30 anger. Anger, when uncontrolled, brings on every kind of physical and spiritual damage.

Still another area in the life of a person who needs a mammoth amount of discipline is sexual passion. The abuse of sexual feelings dominates life in today's world. These could
35 be triggered almost instantly with what enters the mind through the bodily senses. Lacking discipline, a person's life

can go haywire physically, emotionally, and for certain, spiritually. In this age, sexual stimulations are blatantly presented through the media, the world of entertainment, advertisements, and the general milieu of associations. Our "civilized" society has gone deeper in depravity than any other society in the history of humanity. Advances in technology have placed obscenity and pornography in every home. This is the climate in which we live. Unless one makes a resolve to discipline and to tap into sources of grace, salvation of one's soul can be in serious danger. You need to stand guard over all the intake of your entire human system. Stimulations are presented to your eyes, your ears, and your memories, at work and with friends. They come at you with a powerful force. What to do? You have the responsibility to God and to yourself to stand sentinel over your eyes, ears, and over all the other sources of sexual perversion that are thrown at you from all sides. It begins with the question, "Do I want this? Should I want this?" It does come down to a question; how much do God's commands mean to you? "Should I take what I want?" "Do God's wishes mean anything to me?" Your answer to these, will make the difference whether you will call upon discipline or not. If you tap into your heart, bring out the power of discipline and set out to attack impure thoughts, you stand the chance of overpowering these thoughts, and feelings. Thus you prevent yourself from consenting to an offense against purity. The match must be extinguished before it burns down the entire building. Our Lady is asking of purity of heart. It's a challenge to respond to her request. You can lick the depraved and immoral serpent that forcefully demands entrance with discipline and with the help of prayer, and especially with the help of the Holy Spirit and His Spouse, the pure Virgin Mary.

Food intake is another area in which discipline comes in handy. Do I eat to live, or do I live to eat? Our supermarkets are so arranged and filled with such enticements that it is next to impossible to get on the scale without always being shocked. The mind can be a hindrance. It can be an associate. With the help of discipline and the grace from above, the mind can come up with, "No, I don't need to eat now. I just ate two hours ago." Then comes the will. "OK, if I don't need it, why eat it?" Did God give us our taste buds and enormous selection of fruits and vegetables and other foods so that we would gorge ourselves or did He do so in order for us to sustain ourselves in life?

What would you gain from your prayer life if you could not exercise discipline over your thoughts? On a human level, if while you were conversing with someone some other person passed by and you abruptly interrupted your conversation to give attention to the passerby. It would be the height of rudeness. It is the same in prayer. While you are conversing with God, all other thoughts would be a rude intrusion into your conversation. If you truly want to talk with God, each time a distraction enters into your mind, common decency would require that you would abruptly eject the interrupting thought. It all depends on the condition of your will. If you have a strong will you could banish the intruding thought immediately.

One act of discipline in any of the above areas will help you to be in charge of any or every intake that is thrown out for your consumption. Each time that the will can say, NO! it gets stronger. The wills of all the people in the entire world have been damaged by Satan. He has used his subtle and cunning ways to keep us in the head so that we completely forget that we have the will and has arranged conditions down through the centuries so that humans become soft and enervated of will so that they can even lose will to live. He does not want you to be disciplined. He does not want you or me to find the will, and surely he does not want the will to be strengthened. He loses out. Satan is rendered inoperative when one is in charge of his own will. He may not by God's orders enter one's will. He is clever though. He enters into the mind, from the mind to the feelings, and from the feelings to action. He has power over people through their feelings. Statistically, more people live by their feelings than by any other force. The will is the highest faculty from which to launch into action, the will and the mind working together form an integral team. When a person simply does what he/she feels like, such a person misses the whole purpose of life.

With what you have read thus far, you can already begin to hope that it is possible for you to reach a plateau of life that is uncommon in our day taking each step with deliberateness, with patience, but with steadfastness. Conversions or transformations do not come about instantly. Step-by-step, patiently, moving ahead with the help of all of Heaven, your life can be of higher caliber. It is you and you alone who can make the difference on what level of life you will live. Allow yourself to trust that it can be done and YOU can do it with the help of God's grace. It all starts with a disciplined life. God, the Holy Spirit, is ready and willing to help you all along the way, from start to finish.

CHAPTER 18

Your Heart and the Experience of Absorption

"Take My yoke upon you and learn from Me, for I am meek and humble of heart, and you will find rest for yourselves. For My yoke is easy and My burden light."

(Matt. 11:29-30)

Bounty, the paper towel, is a household item famously advertised for its power of absorption. Spill a glass of milk on the counter, apply Bounty and presto, all cleaned up. The subject of this chapter centers around the heart with its own unique quality of absorption. God knew that when He created human beings that they would have a lot of sorrow, heartaches, and setbacks. So when He created their hearts, He made them in such a way that they could absorb whatever they had to endure during their lifetime. The mind, on the other hand, absorbs knowledge and can retain information. It is not however able to absorb difficulties. It can figure out ways to get around them but it is not able to absorb as can the heart. This is an enormous gift from God. especially because it makes the ups and downs of life much more digestible.

You have probably heard various expressions by which the heart with its specific qualities can be better known. There is the loving heart, the believing heart, the joyful heart, and the like. One particular distinction concerns us here. There is hard heart and there is the soft heart. Another way that this is at times spoken of is the warm heart and the cold heart. The soft heart is the warm heart; the hard heart is the cold heart. Did you ever wonder what made the difference in people? Why are some people so cold-hearted? Why among your friends do you find those who have a hard heart, and those with a soft heart? Just what makes the difference?

This distinction is important in our dealing with the absorptive qualities of the heart because you can understand clearly that the hard heart certainly cannot absorb. If you would take a pork chop out of the freezer, you know that it cannot be consumed until it thaws out. The Lord told us by way of His prophet, "I will give them one heart, and put a new spirit within them. I will take the stony heart out of their flesh and give them a heart of flesh."(Ezek. 11:19)God is lamenting over His Chosen People, because they had turned away from Him. Their hearts had become cold and hardened. They did not follow out His laws or keep His decrees. This is the clue. This is the reason why there are people whose hearts would be absorptive but are not because they do not follow the Commandments of God in their lives.

⁵ Obedience makes the heart soft and warm; disobedience makes it hard and cold. The more obedient the heart, the warmer and softer it becomes and the better absorbing power it has. Conversely, the more disobedient the heart, the colder and harder it becomes. It follows that a person who is self-¹⁰ centered, keeps his heart to himself instead of giving it over to God, to Whom it really belongs. The soft heart can absorb pain much better. It can be said logically that the disobedient person suffers more because pain cannot penetrate a hardened heart. An obedient person can take on greater pain ¹⁵ because obedience renders the heart soft and so it has the power of greater absorption. Herein we find an instant punishment for disobedience and an instant reward for obedience.

Anything works better if it is used for the purpose for which it was made. If a man in his workshop cannot put his hands ²⁰ immediately on his hammer and settles to hit a nail with the handle of a screwdriver, he does not get the job done well and may even do damage to the screwdriver. If a person is not obedient, as all human beings were created to be, such a one is going through life with a hardened heart. He is bound to do ²⁵ damage to his heart physically and spiritually.

There are marvelous benefits that flow into the heart of the obedient person. The first is that of a fine-tuned heart; a heart that is tender, sensitive, and thoroughly resilient. The heart is gentle and above all very adept to receive graces from God. An ³⁰ obedient heart is highly receptive to the influxes of the Holy Spirit. It is easily impressed by Him so that it can quickly attain the virtuous life displayed by Jesus. It readily accepts all the love that the Holy Spirit, Jesus, the Father, and Mary are eager to share with it. When it receives love in abundance, it is ready ³⁵ to return love for love and it is generous with its love to all the people it encounters in everyday life.

The soft heart is quick to give and docile in giving loving service to God and to all of His Family in heaven. It readily reaches out to the Souls in Purgatory. It generously undertakes a ministry of dispensing the overflow of its love through the corporal and spiritual works of mercy. It is perfectly attuned to all of the beatitudes. It is outgoing by nature and sensitive to the needs and pains of all. Its mercy and compassion are of a high quality, going forth freely to touch other hearts with its warmth. It is keenly tuned into the Will of God and ready and willing to follow whatever of God's wishes it perceives. It graciously overlooks the faults of others and always tends to find the good points within them.

The heart in its softness skillfully absorbs inconveniences, setbacks, and all types of pain. Accepting willfully whatever crosses God places upon it, the heart can take intense pain with courage. It is the kind of heart found within souls who gave their very best gift to God through martyrdom. In its stance of obedience, the absorptive heart elicits a joyful 'yes' to whatever it encounters on its life's path be it that which gives joy or that which pours forth sorrow. It never allows itself to hit the highest heights of joy nor to go into the pits of sadness. There is a radiance of face, a glitter in the eyes, and a song in heart even when under extensive pressures and responsibilities. The heart has the limitless capacity to receive whatever graces God wishes to bestow upon it, and as it receives graces, it responds in gratitude and turns around to share those graces with others. As it receives, so in its resilience it gives. God is willing to use the absorptive heart to serve as a channel of grace for other souls for He has tested this heart and finds that it does not hoard anything to itself but is genuinely detached from all that it receives and gives generously to others without strings attached. God always finds it ready to receive new gifts.

For the good of all humankind, God, from the beginning of time selected certain individuals to share in His redemptive mission by giving to Himself a countless number of victim souls. These souls with their absorptive heart are capable of heroic suffering. There is no measurement of pain by the mind. The mind is kept in abeyance so that the soul living in a deep state of belief and trust, has no self-reflection, but with its obedient heart depends only on God's wish as to the intensity and the quality of its suffering.

There is another level of life that the absorptive soul is proficient in handling with the expertise of a saint. It is the level on which are found such sufferings as slander, criticism, ridicule, rejection, abandonment by family, friends, and even by members of the Faith, lay and clerical. It is capable of handling accusations, lies, rebuffs, misunderstanding, and all the characteristics which a soul would want to have so that it could maintain its self-respect. It harbors no resentments, no revenge, no ill will. One can see in this heart the heart of Jesus as He took upon Himself the disdain of those whom He came to redeem.

Yes, the soft, warm heart is such not only because of its obedient life but also for what God does for an obedient soul — fill it with all sorts of gifts. Because the soul lives for God and often on the level of living in God, God lives in the soul and transmits His qualities through the soul. It is what St. Paul speaks of when speaking of himself said, "It is no longer I that live, but Christ lives in me." (Gal. 2:20)

You may bristle a bit, dear heart, and say, "Whoa, hold it. That is no life for me. I'm still only with the five-decade rosary and get in an occasional daily Mass. That life is way out there somewhere with those who are exceptional." It may be somewhat threatening, but you never know what God would do for you given the opportunity. We are our own worst enemies. We tend to sell ourselves short. The absorptive heart is a happy heart. It is true that many people cannot stand prosperity. They never had it and are uncomfortable even at the possibility of having it. It is even difficult for some people to receive ordinary love. They wouldn't know what to do with it if it should come their way.

There is a colorful one-liner which hits the spot here. In baseball, the pitcher never pitches until the catcher is ready to catch. God cannot give you His gifts unless you are ready to accept them. For you to give a bit of extra joy to the Lord, you might try this for size: "Lord, if you want to bless me, you may." If you watch to see if He is going to bless you, He won't. He will take you up on your request only if it comes from your heart.

As you travel on this journey, you just might be surprised by a gift or two which crept into your soul without you even being aware of it. God does things like that. When He observes you struggling on the road from the head to the heart, you may touch His Heart when He sees your sincerity and stick-to-it quality. He may just take the liberty to give you unsolicited blessings. So be it. Take your chances. Be ready for anything, though; God is full of surprises. I do know one thing. Once you have finished your journey you will become more mellow, and after that the sky is the limit as to what God will choose to do for you.

CHAPTER 19

Your Heart and the Experience of Generosity

"From his fullness we have all received grace in place of grace."
(John 1:16)

"Cure the sick, raise the dead, cleanse lepers, drive out demons. Without cost you have received; without cost you are to give."
(Matt. 10:8)

*T*here is no generosity greater than the generosity of God. If this is so, why is it that billions of people know nothing about it? It is because they do not slow down enough to take stock and see what is going on around them. It is because through fallen human nature they center their lives around themselves. It is because they have not heard of Jesus nor have they learned about the generosity of their God from anyone. In the final analysis, no one has given the example of generosity to them.

There is a generosity that is of human origin. You do meet people who, not knowing Jesus, would nevertheless give you the shirt off their back. These are people of good will who are not far from the kingdom. Because of their human generosity, once their soul is further disposed, the grace of God will touch them. They will be moved to find Jesus.

Do you recall that episode written in Sacred Scripture when Jesus asked His disciples the question of who do the people say is the Son of Man? Do you also recall when He put it right to them and wanted to know what do THEY say? The point being made here concerns your own awareness of God's generosity. It is not a matter of heart to be aware of God's generosity. It is the task of the mind to point out to you the quality of your own generosity.

By now you are fully aware that you are not your own. You, yourself, are an object of God's generosity. You would never have had the opportunity to experience life except for His generosity. He has put you into a universe that totally reflects this quality of generosity in His Being. Just consider the number of stars in the heavens, the variety of climates on earth, the many, many human beings He has created. This is only a start. Everything in the world is like one huge horn of plenty with numberless kinds of fruits, vegetables, animals, flowers, plants, trees, birds, and fish. Every continent has its own unique varieties of these. Would you imagine that God is generous even in the crosses He permits His people to carry? He does this in order to keep them humble. God's generosity is absolutely awesome! Given the opportunity, the mind cannot help but become aware of the greatness of the Heart of its Maker.

If you take the time and make the effort, you can allow your-self to be absolutely stunned at the extent of God's goodness in giving to His people anything and everything that would help them to accomplish the purpose for which they had been placed on the earth. Consider the history of His Chosen People from the time of Abraham to the coming of Jesus, the Redeemer. Observe the goodness of God and His tremendous largess as you leaf through the pages of the Gospels and are made aware of all that Jesus said and did. Every word and act is the fruit of the outpouring of His love in generosity for His people. From the Cross, He gives His Mother. Before leaving the world, He gives the Holy Spirit. There is always more.

In this very time of yours, in preparing for the Second Coming of Jesus, behold the generosity of the Triune God in the effort that is being made to prepare His people. Each of the Three Persons had a part in the decision to send Mary into our midst and she, as any good mother, is giving Herself totally to Her children on earth in following out the generous wishes of Her Father, Her Son, Her Spouse. Do become aware of the continuous flow of the Father's mercy on this age on which His justice should have been meted out years ago, as indicated by His actions in the past toward other ages of evil fame. Hopefully you are mindful of the stream of God's graces coming through apparitions, locution, prayer groups, Eucharistic miracles and perpetual adoration. All of the above and even more are expressions of God's generosity in your own day. They are given for you to observe, to give witness to, and to make use of.

You are a child of your Heavenly Father and a brother or sister of your Big Brother. You are to learn from them and become more generous yourself. I suspect that you are already in your heart as you have traveled many hours on the journey from your head. Being already in the heart, you can experience your own generosity that comes from within it. Allow yourself joy over this. It gives evidence to the fact that you are not completely absorbed in yourself, that your vision of life is obviously beyond your own self. Presently, it is only a challenge for you to grow in generosity that gradually you can become even more like Jesus. The world needs you to give witness to a generosity of heroic kind.

In my many years of counseling, I have found the absence of generosity within the family structure alarming. It begins with Mom and Dad. If the children do not see generosity expressed between them, the lesson doesn't stick. It is true that in every family, there are many complicated situations that arise unexpectedly. The answer is to keep your generosity motor running all the time. If through prayer and practice you become a generous person, instead of doing generous things once in awhile, your generosity will be always with you.

What a beautiful sight it is when two people who have lived in marriage for some forty or fifty years with all of the ups and downs, are nonetheless cordial, reverential, and generous to each other in their older days. When the children are out on their own and their physical condition begins to weaken, the years of generosity that have preceded conditions of ill health, will be the ointment that will do more good than all the medicines, canes, and walkers they need to make use of in their remaining years together.

How does one grow in generosity? The instant answer that comes up so often on this your journey is to reach out to the Holy Spirit. He will give you details of this growth that are just for you. He knows you better than anyone else. He knows your pluses and your minuses. He knows exactly where your very next step is in your attainment of a greater degree of generosity. You do know that it requires a stretching of your generosity muscles. By His power you will have the courage, the power, and the incentive to go out of your state of comfortable giving, to that which will demand greater sacrifices than you are already making. All of this will become easy under His guidance and power. Depend on His Wisdom and Energy rather than on you own.

This is such an important subject that it might be best for you to take a rest from reading. Pull away to be by yourself, and utter a sincere prayer for growth in your own personal generosity toward God, yourself, your family and friends.

CHAPTER 20

Your Heart and the Experience of Detachment

> *"Whoever loves father or mother more than Me is not worthy of Me, and whoever loves son or daughter more that Me is not worthy of Me, and whoever does not take up his cross and follow after Me is not worthy of Me. Whoever finds his life will lose it, and whoever loses his life for My sake will find it."*
>
> *(Matt. 10:37-39)*

*D*etachment is an experience of the heart. It is the process of making itself free of all attachments to self, in order to become totally committed to the Father as its Creator, to Jesus as its Redeemer, to the Holy Spirit as its
5 Sanctifier.

Why does the heart need detachment from self? It needs to be detached from self because it, in its natural state, is so attached to self that it cannot go beyond itself to accomplish what it was put on earth to do. It was put on earth to get to
10 know God so that it could fall in love with Him and, falling in love with Him, that it would serve Him so that in the final analysis it could spend an eternity of happiness with Him. Both the heart with the head need to work together in order for the soul to experience total detachment. To take the first step of
15 getting to know God, it is primarily the task of the head although the head needs the help of the heart. The second step, falling in love with Him, is primarily the task of the heart although the heart needs the help of the head. Finally, once the soul loves God, both the head and the heart work together
20 to give God loving service by giving loving service to all of His creatures.

Following through the above sequence would be a very simple thing to do, if it were not that each human, since the time our first parents sinned, has come into the world
25 damaged. The mind of the soul enters life darkened, the will weakened, the body disordered. The composite of body, mind and will are disoriented. Rather than tending toward God, even to get through the first step, it becomes not only a hardship but also comes close to an impossibility for anyone like
30 yourself to get beyond self. Man, because of this handicapped condition has become glued to himself and can scarcely make the effort to make his way to find God, much less to love and serve Him. Man comes into the world being self-centered. The challenge of his lifetime is ultimately to become God-
35 centered. The process of detachment aims to do just that.

Both the body and soul must be involved in this process. The greatest burden lies with the heart.

The fallen condition of mankind, as we may call it, came about almost at the very creation of mankind. Adam and Eve from whom the entire human race has had its origin, failed God. At the instigation of the fallen Lucifer, our first parents were tricked into taking their glance away from God in their life of obedience, and to put it onto themselves. Both Lucifer, his follower angels, and Adam and Eve used the power of free choice given to them in their creation to choose themselves over God. God did not want to be served by force. He wanted angels and humans to choose freely to serve Him. This is what is expressed by love. As long as these particular angels and these two human beings chose to live for themselves rather than for God, the angels were cast into hell. Adam and Eve were deprived of their happy abode in paradise only to live on earth earning their bread by the sweat of their brow. They lost their original orientation of putting God first in their life as did all of their posterity.

There was a happy ending to part of the above. Human beings were given a second chance. This was not so however with the fallen angels. God offered this second chance when He sent to earth a Messiah. He would come to reestablish the orientation lost for mankind by Adam and Eve. The Messiah came some two thousand years ago and arranged that anyone who would follow His directives could gain what was lost and, finally, make it possible to enjoy an eternity of happiness with God. At this very moment, you and I, dear reader, as all of our brothers and sisters all over the world have the opportunity for salvation provided we do as Jesus, the Messiah, directs.

Jesus is the Son of God made Man. Jesus is God. Jesus is Man. He is the bridge between humans and the Father. Jesus gave Himself to the Father in our stead by suffering and dying to atone to the Father for the damage caused by our first parents. While on earth, He not only set forth the path man must follow but He also offered mankind the Holy Spirit and gave it the service of His Mother. In addition, He established a living structure within which human beings were to enter and to live so as finally to be able to put God first in their life. Through this living structure, the Church, all human beings were promised safe arrival to the gates of heaven where they were to take up their abode with God in total happiness for all eternity.

Human beings enter into life handicapped. However, because Jesus earned a second chance for mankind, when a child receives the Sacrament of Baptism the child's soul is elevated from a natural state to a supernatural state. As the child grows receiving the helps and graces offered within the Church with the use of the Sacraments, that child is able to learn how to detach itself from the world and attach itself to God. Through the training received within the Church, the child learns how to make its way through life in such a way that it is able to enter into the presence of God in heaven at death.

All the above long, but necessary, is offered as the foundation for this consideration of detachment. Though God through Jesus has offered us salvation, we must show by our actions that we accept it. Jesus earned heaven for human beings but each human being is now on his/her own to follow Jesus toward eternal salvation. You and I have the personal responsibility to make use of whatever Jesus has offered to make it through this valley of tears and to regain for ourselves what has been lost for us through the sin of our first parents.

What still needs to be said is that the STAIN of Original Sin is washed away from individuals who are baptized however, the EFFECTS of Original Sin still remain. The mind of man is still darkened and his will is still weak. The hopeful fact is that we, taking the prescriptions of Jesus to heart, can have our minds enlightened and our wills strengthened. We will be able to make it to our final destiny despite the fact that there is still within each human being an INCLINATION to revert to our darkened and weakened state. We have means, however, offered us that are powerful enough to overpower this inclination. One of these means is penance, by which we can declare war on the effects of Original Sin by weakening the inclination to fall back into our original state, even though we have been elevated to a state of friendship with God through Baptism. This inclination to self-centeredness will be with us until death. It is something we have to live with and yet something that can be overcome provided effort is made. Working on detachment from self is part of that effort.

What is involved in detachment? Detachment involves everything that short-circuits a total commitment to God. Any activity that glorifies self instead of God must be the prime target of detachment. Detachment means "an ungluing from." A certain violence has to be directed against anything and anyone who would stand in the way of putting God first in one's life. This could include anything from a sinful relationship to an inordinate craving for sweets. There are extremely severe forces that keep one fixed to self. There are severe forces, medium forces, and slight forces. There are a tremendous variety of objects that could keep a person at a greater or lesser distance from attaining the goal of pivoting one's life around God.

Pride is at the root of all attachments. To take the axe and cut into the trunk of a diseased tree is easier than taking it down branch by branch. If you would declare war against the pride that you may find within you, it would do away with many obstacles to a total commitment. What is pride? Pride is essentially setting oneself above God. It is when one considers himself/herself better than others. It shows up when I think first of myself and give others very little or no thought. It is found in the statement, "If I don't take care of myself, no one else will." It is expressed when an individual elbows his/her way through, to what is best for the individual taking no heed that he/she is walking over or destroying anyone who gets in the way. Pride shines clearly through one's ego drive by which a person forges ahead without consideration for the welfare of others. One suffers from pride when the internal eye is so swollen that it can see no one else but oneself. I think you get the idea. Our civilization is tainted, not so much tainted perhaps as coming to an utter destruction through the terminal cancer of "me-ism."

Prayer is the best remedy here. Real, deep, honest to goodness, prayer within which one storms heaven with the urgent plea for deliverance. Fasting is very powerful. These two weapons may have to be used even for a person to admit that pride is present within one's soul. Pride is blind and can be very deceptive. Satan gets in on this one and helps the person to rationalize his/her motives and behavior. The Holy Spirit is a skillful surgeon. The problem of pride, once given over to Him, will quickly be recycled into remorse and humility.

From pride flows every kind of sin, aberration, and perversion. It needs the greatest of spiritual guns to trim it to the size of a valid self-respect. In the world today, only a small segment of the population would have an interest in doing something to counter this egocentric mania. Most consider it a necessity for self-survival. For you even to be reading this chapter is a minor miracle of grace that has been given to you. Satan who is "pride personified," has so dealt with this generation that God Personally will have to come to its rescue and pull it out of the fire of pride to make it fit for salvation. It will come to be a battle between the proud and the humble. Only because God will be on the side of the humble will there be the smallest chance that the remnant can overcome the powerhouse force of pride. It might be interesting for you to know that once Satan is defeated, it will not be by the force of power. It will be by an army of humble people connected with Mary, who has been destined by God to crush the head of the serpent. It will not be by her own power but through her humble calling as the Handmaid of the Lord.

After pride, the body is the next huge detriment to a loving relationship with God. Its cravings, passions, and want of comfort is the soul's number one headache as it strives to draw close to God. The eyes want to see everything; the ears crave for the latest bit of juicy stuff; the stomach seeks ever to be overfilled. The palate seeks the most exotic of tastes. The sexual appetite, stimulated by the sex-addicted pagan climate, ever clamors to be satisfied. I don't think any of this has to be elaborated upon. The situation that every Christian is in, with regard to the flesh, is well known and the antidotes are freely offered especially by Our Lady. She asks for penance, prayer and fasting. When these are undertaken by way of the prompts of the Holy Spirit, or out of obedience to Mother Mary, they are powerful enough to bring the body down to size literally and otherwise. One must not fall into the heresies of the past. The body is not evil. God made it and it is the temple of the Holy Spirit. It does have a tendency to go overboard. It needs the firm "hand" of the heart to keep its desires in check. Everything in moderation.

It is no wonder that the body offers detachment problems even to us as Christians wishing to give ourselves to God with our whole hearts. The media presents the body as a god. The advertising, as I am sure you are aware, is unbelievable. It's all body, body, body. No importance is given to the more important part of the human being, the soul. It is no surprise. We are living in a pagan country. As a way to work against the deification of flesh, give respect to the body that truly belongs not to you but to God. He does want you to take care of it. Be kind and understanding to it. Give it the care it deserves as the house for the soul.

The mind needs help with detachment. It craves to have its curiosity satisfied. It wants to know what people say, what they wear, what they do. It has a part in a somewhat big obstacle to a Christ-centered life. It caters to human respect, almost to the level of a cult of pleasing people. It is an effort on the part of any individual not to be a people pleaser in order to experience acceptance and recognition by them.

To achieve within the soul a freedom that comes from detachment, an effort should be put into the enlivenment of conscience. Conscience is a gift from God to help you to do good and avoid evil. There are so many opinions thrown at you, it is no wonder that confusion sets in as to what is really right and what is really wrong. There is within you, as within all people, a sense of right and wrong. Satan has been tampering with values so as to unsettle people who have been living with the Christian code of ethics. It no longer seems possible to have a clear-cut knowledge of objective right and wrong. In the pluralistic society within which you circulate, you can easily be swayed by misguided theologians unless your value system is deeply rooted within you. With a sensitive conscience, you will be able to detect that which leads you toward God and that which leads you away.

Working with detachment is serious business. It is not a matter of, "It would be nice if I could avoid this or give up that … " If your body knows that you are soft on it, it will take you for what it can. If the cravings of your body speak louder than your conscience, your conscience may need an overhauling. The Lord was tough on the things that lead away from God. Recall what He said about riches, violence to the scandalizing eye and hand; about violence to enter the kingdom. He is not encouraging ruthlessness, but He is encouraging you to be firm with yourself, so that you take responsibility over your body with its five senses, and over your soul, with its head and its heart. Recognize what in you is your enemy, and with courage root it out. Earth is not meant to be heaven. If too much emphasis is placed upon what can be squeezed out of it for gratification, one could lose sight of the real heaven. The practice of prudent detachment from those attachments of body and soul, which should be taken care of without procrastination. It is wise to start with the little things that are enslaving and gradually get enough courage to tackle those which are larger. With the help of the Holy Spirit, you will find that a life of detachment is very rewarding. Detachment will never be popular but it will always be necessary. The saying goes, "Make hay while the sun shines." It is a time of mercy, a time of grace. With the help of all in heaven, clear everything out of the way which keeps you from totally committing yourself to the Blessed Trinity.

CHAPTER 21

Your Heart and the Experience of Surrender

"Should anyone press you into service for one mile, go with him for two miles. Give to the one who asks of you, and do not turn your back on one who wants to borrow."

(5:41-42)

"Jesus called out with a loud voice, 'Father, into your hands I commit My spirit.' and when he had said this, He breathed His last."

(Luke 23:46)

When I was very young and played with children of my age, we would get into wrestling bouts. We would go at it until one or the other was pinned down and could not move. With gusto, the one who was on top victoriously shouted "SURRENDER?" The loser, with desperation coated with shame, said, "Yes." It was not a very manly feeling to be pinned down with a crowd watching. Jesus had that feeling pinned to the Cross. After three hours, He gave in, not as the loser but as the winner. How could He be a winner, when in the values of the world of His day, His life was snuffed out of Him by His enemies. It was because He surrendered to His Father and not to His enemies.

You and I came into life in the state of surrender. When we left the comfortable home of nine months and made our debut onto the world stage, naked and helpless, God in His Kindness allowed our self-consciousness to remain undeveloped. It's a good thing because if we were self conscious we might have, out of propriety, refused to move from our nine month private abode. Who, in their right mind, would ever choose to make a presentation under those same conditions with people you never saw before waiting to take a look at you in the helpless condition of birth.

For good reasons, God arranged that the human mind not develop until later; much later, after birth. Every member of the human race comes into life completely dependent upon others. That dependence remains for some years. Even when a child is old enough to go to school, it is still dependent and lives in the state of surrender to those adults around it. This situation exists for many years. When that young adult comes of age, the inner craving for one's own thoughts and the experience of freedom, can finally be enjoyed. Ordinarily young animals will depend upon their mothers for just a very short time and then independently go off on their own. This is not the case for young humans Why?

God knows why. You and I can guess. To consider it logically, it would seem that what God wanted was for each person to learn goodness first. Before the child could acquire a mind of its own, it had to depend on the mind of others. It had to learn by being taught by others. It was formed by the time it could generate its own thoughts. Psychologists tell us that. The child lives in the state of surrender long before it experiences the state of thought.

God must see something good in the state of human surrender. It may be to God's benefit and it may be for the benefit of the human. Given the belief that no man is an island, that each infant was ushered into life within the framework of a family and as a member of society, he/she would always have to live in the state of surrender whether it was something to be merely tolerated or not. The human being is a creature of surrender whether one is ready and willing to admit it or not. It's a fact! The wild horse has to be broken; the independent streak within a human being has to be conditioned.

According to Jesus' teaching, a person's individuality is respected to the degree that one is given personal responsibilities. He presents it when He speaks of the parable of the talents. One gets two, he is expected to return the two and two more. Another gets five, he must produce an extra five... and you know the rest. He also points out that each individual will have to stand before the Judge to give an account of his behavior. It becomes evident that whether I am an individual as an individual or an individual within a community, I must experience surrender. It should be concluded that, as human beings, we have been made in order to live in a harness of surrender. I may never be my own person because I did not make me and I do not belong to me. My individuality needs for me to live in surrender to other humans. It needs, likewise, to live in surrender to its Maker. To live in surrender to my Maker, I need to live in surrender to other humans.

The human condition may look quite bleak to the honest observer. It does not look bleak at all to God. He holds the answer to the riddle of humans being born free and yet not permitted to live freely. He offers this solution to the riddle:

"Then you will know the truth, and the truth will set you free." (John 8:32) The truth is that human beings, through the courtesy of Jesus. are not slaves but friends. God is a Friend. He does not exert authority over humans as a master does over slaves. Scriptural theology upgrades humans when it points out that Jesus is a Brother to each human being and that through the power of the Holy Spirit, each human being has God as an "Abba" or "Daddy."

The experience of surrender within the human heart is not the suffocating surrender of a slave. It is the liberating surrender of a friend or a child to a loving Father. It is a form of real but not forced surrender. What is it then that makes a person who lives in surrender a free person? Take a good note of this response. It is when a person lives in LOVING surrender. That's IT! It's the loving surrender of the child to its parents. It is the loving surrender of a wife to her husband. It is the loving surrender of the husband to God, through which he cherishes his wife and treats her lovingly.

Your heart will experience happiness when it surrenders lovingly to those who deserve your surrender. If this is the way your heart was created by God, so be it. If the truth of this is accepted by your heart and your heart freely chooses to live by this truth, it is a free heart; in its freedom it experiences a joy that nothing in the entire world can compare with. If your heart finds the highest grade of joy known in the world by choosing to live in loving surrender, then that's the way that God intended life to be.

As your heart surrenders lovingly to its Father in heaven and the Father requests of your heart to love everyone, even your enemies, then there will be joy in loving even your enemy. If there are humans who do not choose to live in loving surrender, this will create a serious division within mankind. This division is something we witness in our human family today. Unfortunately, those who choose to live in loving surrender are in the minority. The majority of the present human family live in slavery without even knowing it.

History has recorded what occurs when there are those who are unhappy slaves living in the proximity of people happily living in loving surrender. It has always been the case that what appeared to be a diabolic hatred arose against the happy minority. It would almost seem that this condition of having such groups living together by way of policy or some kind of an established scientific, political, religious, truth, that the unhappiness of the slaves rises to such a fever pitch that it erupts into hatred and the need for revenge. Strife, wars, ethnic cleansing, massacres, all forms of evil are aroused to the need of those who are unhappy. Slaves have the self-given authority to eliminate all who are not of their ilk. What has happened in the past, and continues to this day, is that the unhappy slaves become evil oppressors of those who are happily engaged in loving surrender to God. It always seemed to end in the evil versus the good, Satan's forces against God's loving remnant. History also exposes a truth that is not readily accepted by a raging majority. Namely, when God joined the ranks of the remnant, the great armies of the pursuing unhappy slaves were crushed. As it happened in the past, it is happening even now and without a doubt will continue to happen as long as some choose lovingly to surrender and others choose not to. What a paradox! Those who wish not to surrender in order to enjoy freedom are they who fall into slavery. Those who freely choose lovingly to surrender find true freedom.

Where does all this lead you to, dear reader? Perhaps into a tailspin, trying to figure it all out. It may invite a second reading or at least a bit of deeper and prayerful thought. I would encourage you not to take five, but, to take ten before you travel on. Take courage, the journey from the head to the heart is getting shorter by the day. As you take ten, remember what I asked of you way at the beginning of the journey. Do not read to know, read to grow.

CHAPTER 22

Your Heart and Its Life with the Holy Spirit

"Then there appeared to them tongues as of fire, which parted and came to rest on each one of them."
(Acts 2:3)

"Guard this rich trust with the help of the Holy Spirit that dwells within us."
(2 Tim 1:14)

*E*verything that you have been able to learn thus far is in preparation for what will be presented now. As is the case when putting up a building, after the foundation is set then comes the super structure. Hopefully, what has been said in the previous chapters has set your mind at ease that it is not under attack but that it has its place in life. As long as it knows its place, it is expected to contribute its part in a person's attaining his/her final destiny.

It is my uppermost conviction that Satan, as long as he cannot tamper with man's free will directly, takes a round about way to influence human behavior. First, he has succeeded in convincing much of mankind that thinking is its most important function and that educating the mind must be one's most important undertaking. He has so arranged man's lifestyle that the entire world is obsessed with the need to know. He has succeeded in convincing the greater part of humanity that knowledge is superior to goodness. Second, he enters into the everyday life of the majority of people through their emotional system. Thoughts are connected with feelings; thus, to live by one's feelings is essentially what constitutes the basis of human behavior in this our modern age. As long as Satan can keep your attention riveted in thought and in feelings, he can keep you out of the area of your heart and deprive you of the many fine experiences of the heart that were previously described. Finally, he has so manipulated life on this planet and especially life within the Catholic Church, that the influence of the Holy Spirit upon the world and upon the faithful has been hindered and continues to be .

From your religious training, you have become aware that Jesus came into our midst in order to redeem us from our sins. What may have been mentioned to you and perhaps never given too much emphasis is the fact that all Three Persons were and continue to be involved in that redemption. Each in a unique way. Atonement on the part of humankind was due to the Father. All of humankind put together could not possibly make up to the Father for the injustice directed against Him by the rebellion of Adam and Eve and through them all of the sins of the whole world for the duration of time. It was Jesus Who agreed to become a Human Being just like any human being, except without sin, so that as God and Man He formed the Bridge between the Father and mankind. The Holy Spirit continues to do His part. It was He Who became the Spouse of the Virgin Mother each cooperating to bring the God-Man into the world. In addition, it was the Holy Spirit Who stayed alongside Jesus all the years of His life and prompted Him in His perfect fulfillment of every wish of the Father. It is the Holy Spirit Who stays with the Church, the Mystical Body of Christ, to illumine the minds and inspire the hearts of the faithful to be humble followers of Jesus. It may interest you to know that the Trinity is still very much involved in doing whatever is necessary to help each redeemed person to reach heaven. Dear reader, that includes you.

As Jesus was preparing to ascend into Heaven, He promised to send the Holy Spirit to illumine the minds of the apostles and all His disciples, and to inflame their hearts so that the fruits of the redemption could be extended to every human being on the face of the earth. Thus, the first to the last created human being has the opportunity to attain an eternity of bliss with the Trinity in heaven. You must remember well what happened when the Holy Spirit descended upon the Apostles and the others in the Upper Room; how from being very timid and shy, they became the valiant crusaders for the Faith. You and I and billions of others have been baptized. The Holy Spirit took up His abode within each of us. Billions of the disciples of Christ have allowed the Holy Spirit's enlightenments and inspirations take greater hold of their souls through Confirmation. Now, here is the question. Why is it that we of the Faith, who have been called to be true disciples of Christ through the Sacrament of Confirmation, are so deadbeat, so laconic, and so void of the qualities that transformed all of those in the Upper Room? Mind you it was the same Spirit in both instances then and in our Confirmation. The answer to this is not that easy to come by.

5   As one who was raised in a faith-filled family, trained in the seminary and have lived my priesthood sincerely for many years, I asked this same question of myself. Why has not the Holy Spirit done for me what He did for them? Years of pondering did not come up with the answer until one day it hit like a thunderbolt. My soul was never ready to receive the Holy Spirit as were the souls of those in the Upper Room. The one
10   hundred and twenty recipients of the special blessings of the Spirit were close to Christ. They watched Him being humiliated. They were very emotionally and spiritually set back at His crucifixion. They spent nine full days in deep prayer. When they were in the place of the Pentecost, they were disposed to
15   receive the Spirit with their WHOLE BEING. That's IT! Their whole being was involved. Even at this very moment, I personally have not been able to do just that. I am working at it but have not yet been able to enjoy the totality of commitment that was theirs.
20   There are a couple of things that have helped me. I would like to share them with you. Perhaps they will help you too. I was delightfully blessed some years ago with a brand-new respect for what it is to be a person. Once it hit me, I was able to give myself genuine respect for the first time in my life. This
25   happened when I was already a priest for some twenty years. Would you believe it? When I began to respect myself for WHO I was, I began to respect every other WHO who crossed my path. I was now able to give tremendous respect to the Holy Spirit, the WHO dwelling within my soul since Baptism.
30   That was a great breakthrough. I could never see myself praying to a Dove, a Wind, a Flame; but when I was finally able to give due recognition to the Holy Spirit within me, I passed from pre-K, to about the seventh grade. Then, there was another problem of not being able to give Him a FACE. I have
35   been able to give a Face to the Father and to Jesus, but not to the Holy Spirit. Again, grace came to my rescue. I have talked

by phone to many people around the country whose faces I have never seen. I had no problem there because I knew that they were persons. I believed that the Spirit could "hear" me talking to Him but for the best of me, I could not hear HIS "voice." Again, I was graced. People who love each other do not always communicate with words. Their hearts speak to each other. Voila! My greatest problems melted away. Would that they so melt for all the people in the world, at least for all the faithful within the Church.

You see, dear heart, most of our own people are not in the heart enough to meet up "heart to Heart" with the Holy Spirit. One can know all about Him mentally but that is not enough. Unless our Catholic faithful get the message that they must enter into the recesses of their HEARTS, they will never be able to receive anywhere near the graces that the early Christians received. It was because of these graces that they were able to give up their lives for Christ. The day is coming when we will once again be hunted down and persecuted unto martyrdom. I know this to be a fact. Unless we, as a people of God, get it through our heads that we should be living in our hearts, it will be easy to rationalize with the enemy and compromise when things begin to get rough even unto martyrdom.

The Holy Spirit is very generous. He will bless you as much as you can stand. He will give you as many gifts as you can handle. The first step for anyone like yourself who is sincere and intent on becoming serious about the full meaning of life is to pull aside and come to task with yourself as you are already doing by taking this journey. The second step is to find your way into the heart to be able to have a personal encounter with the Holy Spirit. The third step is to welcome Him and allow Him to make Himself at home within your inner home, to begin to carry on a person to person conversations in faith, in trust, and in silence. You must exercise detachment from the world, from things of the flesh and from your very self. These are the qualities that will make the heart "fertile" for the gifts which the Spirit brought with Him when He took up His dwelling within you. He could not dispense them as long as you were not disposed to receive them. What is needed is to enjoy a relationship with the Holy Spirit similar to that which Jesus had. A loving relationship cannot be attained unless two hearts are equally committed to each other.

Would you please stop a moment in order to call to mind what you read concerning the experiences of belief, trust, and love? These three qualities are given as gifts to each baptized person. They were given to you. Gifts, however must be unwrapped, opened, and tried on for size. It is an insult to the giver of gifts, if the recipient does not even bother to open them. What a shame to leave unwrapped gifts in a closet for years and years! Perhaps even more than shame, this is a crime against a relationship.

Speaking of gifts, I have one for you. If you accept it and make use of it, it will not only make you happy, but all of heaven as well. You have no doubt absorbed some of the "experience" chapters of your book. In order to give the Holy Spirit a treat, and in order to help you to enter a deeper relationship with Him, decide to accept the following gift. Make Mondays, your believing days; Tuesdays, your trusting days; Wednesdays, your loving days; Thursdays, your obedience days; Fridays, your forgiving days; Saturdays your gratitude days; and Sundays, your reverence and adoration days. If you would spend only two minutes each day experiencing each of these heart qualities, within about two months you will become a believing person, a trusting person, a loving person, an obedient person, a forgiving person, a grateful person, a reverent and adoring person. AND, you will be able to enjoy believing thoughts, trusting thoughts, loving thoughts, obedient thoughts, forgiving thoughts, grateful thoughts, reverent thoughts. That is the whole picture and that is what will make you a whole and holy person. Begin to face the reality that there is more to life than thinking. If you spend all or even most of your time thinking, you are allowing yourself to run on about six of your eighty-four human cylinders. Such a ratio will only give you a "putt, putt, putt," when you get into some of the steep grades of life.

Practice giving the Holy Spirit a place of honor within your heart. Allow Him to be the delightful Guest of your inner home. Allow Him to become your private Energizer, your private and personal and built-in Spiritual Director, your Sanctifier, and your Unifier. He would be honored also to become your private Healer. You can't go wrong. The price is right! It's all yours for one price, one price alone, with no bargaining allowed. The price is THE GIFT OF YOURSELF. He will give Himself totally to you and even help you to match Him.

There are two more short thoughts I would like to share with you and then I will be done — for now. First: The Holy Spirit and the Blessed Mother are Spouses. They worked together to bring Jesus into the world; they are now working together to bring Him in for His glorious return. Any movement within the Church that separates Them will never succeed. If the concentration is on "Mary, Mary, Mary," and the Holy Spirit is left out, the movement will not make it. If the concentration is on "Spirit, Spirit, Spirit," and Mary is left out, the movement is moving toward a dead end. In all movements, it must be Mary and the Spirit.

Finally, you must admit that the Catholic Church has been brought into the intensive care unit because of the confusion, the division, the lack of reverence, the hatred, the disobedience, and the lack of respect. Have no fear; Mary and the Spirit are near. Its condition may appear critical, and so it is, but the Attendants are from out of this world. The Two Master Surgeons are at work with St. Joseph, the Protector of the Church, whose sleeves are rolled up so that he can do his part.

CHAPTER 23

Your Heart and the Gifts of the Holy Spirit

"God added His testimony by signs, wonders, various acts of power, and distribution of the gifts of the Holy Spirit according to His will."

(Heb.2:4)

*B*efore you plunge into this most interesting and enriching material, I would like to divert a bit and share two things with you. First, I want you to become familiar with the phrase, "the outside of your inside." You are to make it distinct from the phrase, "the inside of your inside." Your person resides on the inside of your inside. No one else is permitted to enter that part of you. It is exclusively yours given to you by your Creator as a part of your uniqueness. The Holy Spirit resides on the outside of your inside. He is absolutely distinct from your person. The New Agers are trying to ram pantheism on mankind. This is a major heresy. The Holy Spirit residing within you is distinct from you. He does not flow into you for you to give up your personhood. Mind your unique position and guard it with your life. Satan is trying to dislodge you from it by promoting, through some philosophers, that you are nothing but a bundle of habits. You are you, as God made you absolutely distinct from God. You may enjoy divine qualities, but your person always remains human. Even in heaven, you will still be a human person but one submerged in divine qualities. Even while you are immersed in the Beatific Vision, you still remain a human person. It is essential that you integrate this knowledge into a truth that you live by.

The second point is that you, as a person, have a body and a soul. Your soul is more important than your body but both are very important to God. Your soul has two faculties: the mind and the will or the head and the heart. Each of these have their unique value and are given to you, first, to help you to find your way to heaven with God's help and, once you are in heaven, to enjoy God with your heart, head, soul, and body. The body will be brought up to a glorified state as was the Body of Jesus after His Resurrection.

I share the above with you again with my heart and my head. In no way is this treatise belittling the head. In no way would I even dare to knock the mind by degrading it one iota. I present the contents of this entire volume for one purpose and one purpose alone, that is, to uphold the special dignity of the heart in deference to the deification of the mind which Satan is striving to force upon the entire world. This is exactly what he did to our first parents. He is doing the very same to all of mankind by mass trickery. To confront this evil, Jesus presents Himself to the world as the Sacred HEART. Our Mother Mary presents Herself as the Immaculate HEART. This says a lot. Let me offer you the following quote from the Gospel to substantiate this point. A lawyer posed this question to Jesus, "Teacher, which commandment of the law is the greatest?" Jesus said to him, "You shall love the Lord your God, with all your heart, with all your soul, and with all your mind." (Matt 22:37) Both the head and the heart, being assisted by God's grace, have an EQUAL responsibility to help you to get to heaven. Enough said.

Both of the points above have been offered in preparation for a greater appreciation of the gifts which the Holy Spirit has at His disposal to implant into your head and into your heart. In addition to the theological virtues of belief, trust and love, He has entered your soul to bestow upon you seven other special gifts. They are: Wisdom, Understanding, Knowledge, Counsel, Fear of the Lord, Fortitude, and Piety. Let's take a peek at each one now. You can explore them in depth later when prompted to do so by the Holy Spirit.

WISDOM: Wisdom is that supreme gift of the Holy Spirit wherein the human soul which, immersed in the love of God, looks at all things, human and divine through the eyes of God. It is as if the soul were right within the 'heart' of God looking out on a panoramic view through evaluating what is beheld in the same way that God does. On the human plane it is knowledge that comes from love. The knowledge that comes from love is superior to the knowledge that comes from the head itself. It can be expressed in this way: One who has experienced love has a more perfect knowledge of it than one who has read the definition of love in a dictionary. Bringing it right down to earth: A person who is eating a banana has a more perfect knowledge of it rather than the one who is describing it in words. Wisdom is knowledge offered through the experience of love. There is no true wisdom without love. Wisdom without love is mere knowledge. There is a vast difference between the two.

The gift of wisdom, which the Spirit has ready for, you cannot be imparted to you until and unless you are a lover. You cannot be a lover if you are not in your heart. This gift cannot be enjoyed unless and until you have a genuine love of God. This love of God is the supernatural love given and increased by the Holy Spirit. Were the mind to contain all the knowledge possible on a human level, it would not equal the one sentence of knowledge that comes forth from a loving heart. This is as true on the human level as it is on the divine. All of the knowledge of an Einstein will not amount to a hill of beans compared to the knowledge of a mother who has borne a child and says to that child, "I know what you want and what you need." Can you fathom now the depth of evil that came forth from the mouth of Descartes, when he said so pompously "I think, therefore, I exist?" Can you see now that with this philosophy, taken up by the ilk of the modern-ists, how Satan wiggled himself into the vastness of society? Can you now flavor the full impact of the words of Jesus when He said, "I praise you, Father, Lord of heaven and earth, because you have hidden these things from the wise and learned, and revealed them to little children."? (Matt 11:25) To pray for this gift and to prepare yourself to receive it is better than to spend four years getting a doctorate in computer science, or any one of the worldly skills; unless, of course, they are pursued out of love for mankind which has at heart the loving service to God's people.

UNDERSTANDING: The gift of understanding is the loving knowledge of the things of God, of myself, and of others and how life is to be led in favor of attaining our final destiny of eternal bliss with God in heaven. It is a piercing knowledge, a penetrating knowledge, and an experiential knowledge in a way that one experiences what he/she knows. Remember, I am not talking of natural understanding, but if you can get a whiff of what true human understanding is, you can grasp a clear understanding of this supernatural gift. Someone comes up to you and says, "Boy, I'm all out of breath. I got so tired walking up the hill to your house." You say, "Oh yeah, I understand." You do because you climbed up that same hill many times and you too became tired. In the supernatural sense the soul understands with an internal experience what is found in the Gospels especially the Words of Jesus. One endowed with this gift, can have a clear understanding of His teachings. It is not so much an understanding that is found in the mind alone, but one that permeates the whole soul. It is a gift that makes it possible for one to pick up the Scriptures and gain a piercing appreciation of what is read. This gift presupposes the living out of the theological virtues, of belief, trust, and love.

Why is there such aimless living in our day even among the faithful? Why is it that only the remnant, hidden within the Mantle of the Immaculate Heart, continue against great odds to pray the rosary, adore Jesus in the Eucharist, fast, and the like? It is because of the gift of understanding. Few have it. When a soul accepts this gift from the Holy Spirit, it finds that the fewer words it speaks, the more penetrating they are. There are so few of God's people who are not tainted by the deification of knowledge that Satan spews into the atmosphere. Perhaps, this will throw some light on for you why it is such a blessing for you to be on this journey. When you are able to enter your heart at will — by choice — you place yourself into the same 'room' with the Holy Spirit. Only then can true action begin between Him and you. As long as an individual fails to enter into the sacred chambers of one's heart, the futility of life is endlessly envisioned in the rising and setting of the sun. How many fail to enjoy the benefits of the gift of understanding because they are caught within the web of professional administration.

KNOWLEDGE: Human knowledge is a splendid gift to the human family. God is to be praised for devising it. For the human being to be able to go through the process of learning is indeed a feat that only the infinite Mind of God could first conceive and then bring into an operative reality. From one concept to another in a discursive manner, the mind is able to make comparisons, conclusions, and even projections as to where this particular concept can generate many others. The Gift of knowledge is similar and dissimilar. It is similar in that it, too, is able to enjoy concepts but it is dissimilar in that the process of obtaining them is intuitive rather than discursive. There is no reasoning process that goes along with the gift of supernatural knowledge. What a person knows through the gift of knowledge, he/she knows immediately. It is like a flood light that instantly is switched on and the human mind gifted by this supernatural ability is the observer of what appears to be on a stage already set for comprehension. There is no need to pass from one concept to another.

This knowledge has been termed the "science of the saints." The saints did not have to read and read, study and study. All they would need to do is to enter into a stance of prayer and immediately they would have within their minds a bit of knowledge they never have heard about, or had explained to them, or studied or thought about. It just came. The content of this knowledge would have reference to spiritual things, spiritual values, spiritual conclusions, and spiritual convictions. Take St. Francis of Assisi as one classical example. From a life of riches, he went on to a life of detachment, to a love for and an espousal of poverty, and a love of all creatures in whom he saw the imprint of the Loving Father. He pierced through the image of all created objects as they were seen by the natural eyes and the eyes of the world, and was able to connect them with their Maker. And he was finally able to make use of them as stepping stones to a greater love of God.

Would it not be a source of joy if you were able to possess this supernatural gift? I assure you, dear heart, that if you have received the Sacraments of Baptism and Confirmation the gift is there waiting for you. The ordinary requirements you

already know, to be in the heart, to have a person-to-person meeting with the Holy Spirit, and to allow Him to enliven it within you. Your name is already on it through your reception of the above Sacraments. Genuine hearty prayer is a shortcut.
5   It is not SAYING prayers that prepare you to receive it, it is going into your heart and letting the humble heart ask to open that which is already your gift. Count on the Holy Spirit to help you with this. Your belief and trust in Him will get His attention to you and to your gift of knowledge and help you begin to
10 unwrap it.

COUNSEL: It is not always clear what particular behavior to take on, what decisions to make, and what to do in particular instances. Human prudence is a helper. There is within each one of us, at least it is at our disposal, the ability to enter the
15 mind into a deliberative process which outlines the pro's and the con's, in coming to a definite decision for a particular action. Human prudence is not guaranteed. Many prudent individuals have set out on a venture which was judged very sensible at first and later found it ending up badly. There is also
20 the supernatural gift of prudence wherein an individual can count on spiritual values and help from above to make decisions which best fit the accomplishment of sub-goals in favor of the major goal of reaching heaven. Beyond this supernatural virtue of prudence, is the Holy Spirit's gift of counsel.
25 No deliberations need to be made when this gift is in action. The right thing and the better thing to do comes from above in the sense that it is of divine origin. Actually, it comes from the Holy Spirit. In individual instances, to ask the Spirit for light is still not of this gift. The Spirit is most generous and willing to be
30 of assistance anytime and to be asked by anyone for a bit of instant guidance. The guardian angels are great in this area, as is Jesus, Our Lady, and the other angels and saints. However, the gift of counsel resides in the soul of its recipient as a way of life. It is a continuous "plug in" to the Spirit Who allows His
35 Wisdom to flow through the gifted individual. Who can be so fortunate as to have this royal treatment? It is like having an

"in" with a most influential person to be able to obtain benefits that the ordinary person has no access to.

The gift of Counsel is yours to have. You know the price. It is
high by worldly values, but even in the spiritual realm, you only
get what you pay for. This means that you need to accomplish
certain things to merit this gift. Again, I repeat, it is yours
through the reception of the particular Sacraments. The gift of
self is the shortest way into the opening of your gift of counsel.
I do not wish to put words in your mouth, but here is an
example how you might go about it: "Holy Spirit, I consecrate
myself to You. I give myself to You, as the One Who has the
responsibility to sanctify me, to heal me, to guide me. I place
myself at Your disposal, to do with me what You judge is best
for my soul and what will give glory to Jesus and to the Father.
I become as a blind and deaf person in Your care. What will
continue to be mine is my YES to whatever you say, into whatever direction you send me. I trust in Your Wisdom implicitly,
without question." High price? Yes and no!

FEAR OF THE LORD: This gift is none other than the gift of
reverence. Reverence does have a built in 'fear of the Lord,'
but it is not a fear that should cause one to tremble in the presence of the Lord. It is not the crippling fear that a child has
toward a very angry mother. It is a gentle and mild fearfulness
lest one displease the loving Father Who has been so kind and
generous. The word "reverence" would fit, I think.

There is a quality of respect that naturally appears in people.
A quality that does not really want to hurt another but, many
times, is more self-centered. The gift of Reverence is directly
from the Holy Spirit and it is a way of life for the individual, in
which there is a certain awe for God, for His representatives,
and for whatever else is considered as sacred. The gift of
Reverence has reference also to dealing with oneself as a
person of dignity whose Father is kindly, generous, and just.
His Brother is a King, so he/she is a prince/princess. One's
body is respected because it is the temple of the Holy Spirit.
One's soul is given high regard because it is a very special gift

of the Father. Other persons are respected for the same reasons. Reasons, however, do not enter much into all of this because the gift consists of a built-in quality with which its bearer is continuously looking upward from within a state of lowliness. The truth of Who God is and who I am in reference to Him has, through this gift, become a heart-set of the soul.

FORTITUDE: This gift is precious because it brings fear down to the size that can be overcome. The goodness of the Holy Spirit, but especially His Power, flows into the soul so that it feels no need to fear. It is not the same as boldness. It is not an ego-driven approach. There is a natural fortitude with which some people are gifted but the supernatural gift goes beyond the natural. One gifted with the supernatural gift can go so far as to shed blood for the cause of Christ, His Church, or His Gospel.

To arrive at your eternal destiny is no easy matter. There are hardships and there are dangers. Heaven is a reward for our effort to do the things God insists on: to be just in our dealings with others, to exercise the virtue of charity, and to be humble in obedience. There are enemies whom we encounter on our spiritual journey who would harm us. There is Satan and his minions who would rather see us in hell than in heaven. It is this gift of Fortitude that causes strength to flow into the soul from the Divine Giver. Fallen nature always lurks in the foreground to make fear arise at an instant. Powerful temptations against purity, charity, and justice arise when least expected. To have confidence against the powers of the world, the flesh, and the devil is what this gift renders the soul. It does not invite presumption that God is always there, that the Holy Spirit is right within, or to do something like place one's self into deliberate danger. It is a gentle but powerful flow of strength that stays with the person.

You may have within yourself all of the dispositions spoken of above. You may already be enjoying this gift as you travel on this journey from the head to the heart. You know, and I do too that it is not an easy journey to undertake. Much change is necessary. There are evaluations that must be made. Priorities must be put in order and weakness of will must be strengthened. The Holy Spirit could, at times, dip into a gift assigned to a person by way of His largess and love for the soul, He may just slip in a little of the gift to lure a soul to reach out for its full possession. It may be the case such as yours. He knows your goodwill. He is aware of your good intentions. He is at liberty to dispense your gift of fortitude to you as you need it; even to help you to become prepared to receive it on a full-scale basis. This is hopeful.

PIETY: The gift of piety is not what you think it might be. We speak of a person as being pious. "She is so pious." "I don't know what got into him. All of a sudden he has become quite pious." For many, the word has become synonymous with holiness. If the hands of a person are clasped while the eyes are directed heavenward and the person is in a kneeling position, an observer may be quick to think such a person is pious. It may be but the gift of Piety refers more to one's charity toward others. The external appearance of a person has nothing to do with holiness, at least not necessarily. There is a peacefulness, a meekness, and a gentle demeanor radiating from a holy person. But the basis of the gift of Piety is loving service.

The other gifts of the Holy Spirit have to do with one's own spiritual benefits. The Spirit knows the full circle needed for salvation and enters in that part of which Jesus spoke, "I was hungry, you gave me food, enter into the kingdom... ." The gift of Piety helps in this. It mellows the soul to the needs of others. It strips the person of all self-seeking in its love giving. The gift of Piety makes it quite natural for the recipient to keep his/her eyes out for the needs of others, be these physical or spiritual needs, with a total abandonment of self.

Do not think that you have to activate all of these gifts together or overnight. It is all part of your greater journey that goes beyond the journey from the head to the heart. It is part of the "beyond" of your present journey. From my own

journey, the best suggestion that I can make is: be patient, but to let the Spirit know that you are willing to grow and that whatever it takes, you are ready to dive in. Put yourself into a receptive stance and let it be known to Him that you are avail-
⁵ able for Him in whatever way He deems best. Trust that He WILL take the initiative. You can count on His genuine interest in your spiritual progress. You will find Him to be most coop- erative. He is friendly.

In conclusion, I would like to affix the twelfth and thirteenth
¹⁰ chapters of St. Paul's first letter to the Corinthians, as given in the New International Version. It will speak of additional gifts of the Holy Spirit, some of which you are welcome to look into after your journey. In addition, take some time to pray about the preceding material. It is a bit heavy but a vital part in the
¹⁵ development of your life with the Holy Spirit.

Corinthians Chapter 12

"**1.** Now about spiritual gifts, brothers, I do not want you to be ignorant. **2.** You know that when you were pagans,
²⁰ somehow or other you were influenced and led astray to mute idols. **3.** Therefore I tell you that no one who is speaking by the Spirit of God says, "Jesus be cursed," and no one can say, "Jesus is Lord," except by the Holy Spirit. **4.** There are different kinds of gifts, but the same Spirit. **5.** There are different kinds
²⁵ of service, but the same Spirit. **6.** There are different kinds of working, but the same God works all of them in all men. **7.** Now to each one the manifestation of the Spirit is given for the common good.

8. To one there is given through the Spirit the message of
³⁰ wisdom, to another the message of knowledge by means of the same Spirit, **9.** to another faith by the same Spirit, to another gifts of healing by that one Spirit, **10.** to another mirac- ulous powers, to another prophecy, to another distinguishing between spirits, to another speaking in different kinds of
³⁵ tongues, and to still another the interpretation of tongues. **11.**

All these are the work of one and the same Spirit, and he gives them to each one, just as he determines. **12.** The body is a unit, though it is made up of many parts; and though all its parts are many, they form one body. So it is with Christ. **13.** For we were all baptized by one Spirit into one body— whether Jews or Greeks, slave or free— and we were all given the one Spirit to drink. **14.** Now the body is not made up of one part but of many.

15. If the foot should say, "Because I am not a hand, I do not belong to the body," it would not for that reason cease to be part of the body. **16.** And if the ear should say, "Because I am not an eye, I do not belong to the body," it would not for that reason cease to be part of the body. **17.** If the whole body were an eye, where would the sense of hearing be? If the whole body were an ear, where would the sense of smell be? **18.** But in fact God has arranged the parts in the body, every one of them, just as he wanted them to be. **19.** If they were all one part, where would the body be? **20.** As it is, there are many parts, but one body. **21.** The eye cannot say to the hand, "I don't need you!" And the head cannot say to the feet, "I don't need you!" **22.** On the contrary, those parts of the body that seem to be weaker are indispensable, **23.** and the parts that we think are less honorable we treat with special honor. And the parts that are unpresentable are treated with special modesty, **24.** while our presentable parts need no special treatment. But God has combined the members of the body and has given greater honor to the parts that lacked it, **25.** so that there should be no division in the body, but that its parts should have equal concern for each other. **26.** If one part suffers, every part suffers with it; if one part is honored, every part rejoices with it. **27.** Now you are the body of Christ, and each one of you is a part of it. **28.** And in the church God has appointed first of all apostles, second prophets, third teachers, then workers of miracles, also those having gifts of healing, those able to help others, those with gifts of administration, and those speaking in different kinds of tongues. **29.** Are all apostles? Are all prophets? Are all teachers? Do all work miracles? **30.Do** all have gifts of healing? Do all speak in tongues? Do all interpret? 31 But eagerly desire the greater gifts. And now I will show you the most excellent way."

Corinthians Chapter 13

"**1.** If I speak in the tongues of men and of angels, but have not love, I am only a resounding gong or a clanging cymbal. **2.** If I have the gift of prophecy and can fathom all mysteries and all knowledge, and if I have a faith that can move mountains, but have not love, I am nothing. **3.** If I give all I possess to the poor and surrender my body to the flames, but have not love, I gain nothing. **4.** Love is patient, love is kind. It does not envy, it does not boast, it is not proud. **5.** It is not rude, it is not self-seeking, it is not easily angered, it keeps no record of wrongs. **6.** Love does not delight in evil but rejoices with the truth. **7.** It always protects, always trusts, always hopes, always perseveres. **8.** Love never fails. But where there are prophecies, they will cease; where there are tongues, they will be stilled; where there is knowledge, it will pass away. **9.** For we know in part and we prophesy in part, **10.** but when perfection comes, the imperfect disappears. **11.** When I was a child, I talked like a child, I thought like a child, I reasoned like a child. When I became a man, I put childish ways behind me.

12. Now we see but a poor reflection as in a mirror; then we shall see face to face. Now I know in part; then I shall know fully, even as I am fully known. **13.** And now these three remain: faith, hope and love. But the greatest of these is love."

CHAPTER 24

Your Heart and the Fruits of the Holy Spirit

"In contrast, the fruit of the Spirit is love, joy, peace, patience, kindness, generosity, faithfulness, gentleness, self-control. Against such there is no law. Now those who belong to Christ have crucified their flesh with its passions and desires.

(Gal 5:22-24)

*T*he journey from the head to the heart in its written form can take about two to three days, or for some, a mere overnight. In reality, it takes almost a lifetime. The beginning of the journey is at Baptism. Who knows what goes on in the infant's soul and in the soul of the two-to-seven year old. There is no way of knowing what the Spirit may be doing. The little people are all heart no head. It never ceases to amaze me when Jesus speaks of the little ones, their angels, their wisdom, and their possessing the Kingdom. He said: "I tell you the truth, unless you change and become like little children, you will never enter the kingdom of heaven." (Matt.18:3) Have you ever seen an infant smile in its sleep? I have, many times In a family of thirteen, you get to see that often.

It can be taken as a positive truth that when there is no recognition or respect given to the Holy Spirit from a person who has been baptized, the Holy Spirit does not just sit within that soul "twiddling His Thumbs." He IS Life, He IS Truth, He IS Love, He IS Power. The child belongs to God. It was God Who designed that the child would not become a full rational being too early in life. There is a purpose behind all that God does. No one will ever know how many souls were saved for Heaven simply because there were those who were kept on earth long enough to be able to recognize and respect the Holy Spirit. No one will ever know, at least on this side of Heaven, what took place between the Spirit and a child in its early days, might have had a part in his/her conversion in later days. We have often heard that the formative days of a child begin right in the womb. God has the advantage over that child for several years before the adults can get to it. When that child looks at you without words, with its eyes pinned to yours, you have no idea what is going on behind those eyes. If the child is all heart fresh from the Hands of its Creator and the head does not interfere, God alone knows what He is doing to, for, and within that child. It is with this in mind that, perhaps, when the unborn infants are suffering, God is there to give His Fatherly comfort.

When one gets to the end of the journey from the head to the heart, one finds oneself in the heart, and through the heart back into the head. The head becomes a servant of the heart. The Holy Spirit is in charge of the whole journey from start to finish. Notice what the end of the journey turns out to be like. You may not see the whole picture right at this moment but after our consideration of the fruits of the Spirit, you will become awed that at the conclusion of all His Work with the soul it once again becomes childlike. Had we never changed from childhood to adulthood, it would have eliminated at least one extra change from our lives, as Our Lord said, "Unless you change … "

The entire list of the fruits of the Holy Spirit is a very long one. It is longer within some souls than in others but it seems that each person who has chosen to live a life with the Holy Spirit can be guaranteed twelve fruits. As listed in the catechism, they are: Charity, Joy, Peace, Patience, Goodness, Benignity, Longanimity, Mildness, Faith, Modesty, Continence, and Chastity. It should be noted well that these are not virtues; they are the fruits of virtues. The virtue of charity is not the same as the fruit of charity. The same is to be said of the others. It is as though the virtues flower into fruits as in the plant. The plant begins with the seed, gradually becomes a full-grown plant, and then produces the ultimate of what was contained within the plant all along. The plant no longer needs to grow. It, with its produce, is its ultimate end. It is beautiful to behold as its stands proudly before your eyes believing that it has done a good job.

Let us take a brief tour of the fruits. Understand again that it is not the purpose of this manual to go in depth. This you can do once you have made the floor plan for the process of sanctification.

CHARITY: The Holy Spirit IS Love. It stands to reason when He lives within the soul, and the soul has given itself over to

Him with a generosity that was propelled by the Spirit, the soul reflects the love of the Holy Spirit in a perfect way. It is like looking into the mirror to see the reflections of our own face. It is like that piece of iron engulfed in the fire in a steel-tempering furnace in the city of Pittsburgh. The bit of iron remains itself even as it submerged in the intense blaze of the fire. In the same way the soul is not so completely absorbed by the Flame of Love of the Spirit that it loses its own identity. Nonetheless, it leaves not the slightest doubt about the Source of the love within the soul. The soul itself is permeated with love; it is personified love; the love that already has the flavor of Heaven.

No one will doubt that the human heart is the center of one's life. When the heart gives up, the person's journey on this earth is finished. God made it so. In the same vein, the heart is the center of the spiritual life. There are people who want to argue about this but they may be so immersed in the head that they cannot see that there is anything else but knowledge. Nonetheless, despite all the enemies of the preeminence of the heart, God Himself put it first in His design and continues to put it first through His Holy Spirit. Love is the highest and most perfect experience of the heart. Obedience has a prominence in effect that if one does not obey, one cannot even begin to search for the love of the heart. Heaven is where love reigns. We are being told, too, that once the new era begins and heaven comes closer to earth, the heavenly love will permeate the earth's atmosphere. It will be the time when Jesus will establish His reign upon earth.

The fruit of charity within the soul uses the power of love to make suffering a joy; suffering that is offered for souls and their salvation, and that is part of the redemptive plan of the Father. It might interest you to know that when Jesus was nailed to the Cross with every fiber of His Body quivering in intense pain, His Love for all of us was within His Heart beating with a power that sent that Love to every soul that was created and still to be created till the end of time. The fruit of charity allows its bearer to have that same burning love for souls. There are, in our midst, victim souls who are so filled with this love given by the Spirit that for years they bear the greatest of pain in order that souls might turn to God for forgiveness. Once the fruit of love has the heart submersed within it, it is not an effort for the soul to be charitable. Charitableness fills every single crevice of the soul. It was this kind of soul that was within the body of St. Maximilian Kolbe who died as a martyr in a concentration camp during the Second World War. I believe that it is the same love that permeates the soul of Pope John Paul II.

JOY: When the heart is a loving heart through and through, the fruit of such love is joy. It is a joy that the world cannot produce. It is a joy that is only known in Heaven and comes from there to give warmth and hope to others in this vale of tears. It is not something that is put on. It is something that radiates from within. If you were ever in the presence of a person gifted with this joy, you knew immediately that it was from the Holy Spirit. It is the way God works. In times past and in the present, when evil seems to dominate the world, there are within the world people gifted with this joy as a sign to Satan that God is still in charge. This heavenly joy fills a soul only because the soul is filled with love which is the reflection of Love Who is the Holy Spirit. Hell is a place where the last ounce of love leaves a soul as it enters. There is no love in Hell. There is no joy in Hell. This is a reminder that comes to us from Jesus Himself.

PEACE: When a soul is filled with joy, it is in peace. It is a soul filled with peace. We have heard of peace of mind and peace of heart. This is the peace of God within a person. When a person is inundated with peace, the peace comes through the soul, the heart, the head, through the eyes, through the voice, through the entire body as it walks, eats, works, sleeps. It is a peace that is immediately felt by people in the proximity of a man/woman of peace. Such peace is found in Mother Teresa of Calcutta and in Pope John Paul II. I have had the joy of experiencing this peace from both of these individuals. I know that it is heavenly.

As Jesus was leaving for Heaven, as He promised to send the Paraclete. He also spoke of the peace that He would leave with His followers. He said, "Peace I leave with you; my peace I give to you. I do not give to you as the world gives. Do not let your hearts be troubled or afraid." (John 14:27) Anyone who has some of the peace that Jesus speaks of has an absolute conviction that the world's attempt to bring peace among the nations, is not peace at all. It will never be as long as the world keeps its distance from Christ. There are levels of true peace within a soul just as there are levels of love and levels of joy. The deepest level of all three of these lives within the soul having received them as fruits of the Holy Spirit. If you can recall a piece of lamb which has been marinated, you know that the meat is permeated with a particular flavor. Use that image to think of a soul that is permeated with peace. Such peace not only fills the soul through and through but it radiates right through the physical features of a person. Peace is written over one's face, seen in one's eyes and heard in one's voice. The world needs one more person filled with such peace. Hopefully, it will be you, dear reader. As long as you have gone this far in your reading there are great hopes that the Holy Spirit will have just one more person ready and willing to be under His care. It is God's plan that in our time the Holy Spirit will work with the little people of Our Lady's Cohort so that His Peace will cover the face of the earth.

PATIENCE: The above three fruits of the Holy Spirit put order into a soul's life with regard to the good things in life. The reality of life is that not all things go just the way we would like them to. Life is filled with joys and pains, with gladness and sorrows. Patience, as a fruit of the Holy Spirit, makes suffering not only bearable but it makes one joyful over it. The world would interrupt quickly saying this is nothing other than masochism. The world does not know any better. Precisely because it is the world, it is not expected to know any better.

The world says that a person inflicts pain in order to gain pleasure. The Spirit gives joy to a person who has become resigned
to an unexpected pain. Pleasure is of the world. Joy is of
heaven. There is a world of difference between the two.

Suffering on earth lies within the divine plan. It is a plan that
was inaugurated by God's Mercy. He could snuff it out of existence, as a person snuffs out the light of a candle, but He did
not. As gold is purified by fire, the soul is purified by pain. God
could have forced evil out of existence but, by a more perfect
plan evident to Himself if not to human reason, He chose to
make use of evil in order to strengthen goodness. He allows
the weeds to grow along with the wheat until harvest time. It
is the fruit of the Holy Spirit that makes pain helpful to the soul
itself and to all the souls of the world. Pain borne out of love
brings joy. Pain within the heart of a loved one brings the One
Who Loves closer. As Jesus suffered for all of humankind, the
soul, braced by the divine gift of patience, chooses to suffer
and remains at peace with its suffering in imitation of Christ.

LONGANIMITY: There is a very refined form of suffering that
patience does not cover because this suffering is caused by
some infliction presently felt. There is a pain that the soul
suffers in the absence of something or someone in antici-
pating an arrival. It is expressed in the words of St. Paul when
he speaks of having to be in the midst of the people, yet yearns
to be already in the presence of God. It is the pain that a wife
felt in her heart, as she waited for her husband, a soldier
across the seas, to return to her. On its most sublime level, the
soul is aware of the promises of God that good will triumph
and evil will be defeated. It is a soul that lives in trust that all of
the promises which God has made would be fulfilled. Waiting
for those promises to be fulfilled, a soul is in dire need of the
promises to be fulfilled for its own spiritual benefit. It is a pain
that you, dear heart, could experience in reading all about the
good things of the spirit not yet realized within your own soul
with the hope that somehow God would make it so.

The Holy Spirit sees all and knows all. He is fully aware of the pain that is within each and every soul, as it anticipates getting to confession, as it hopes to enjoy the fullness of freedom and of life. It is why He makes this fruit of longanimity available. This fruit so effects the soul that, even in the depth of pain, the soul is at peace and is experiencing joy. It is not anything that the soul psyches itself into, it is given by the Spirit as an assistance. It is also given as a reward for the life of goodness that the soul is already engaged in. The Holy Spirit continues to be Love in being generous to souls; His Love goes out to the persons who not only need to be in pain for purification sake but wish to be in pain for love's sake. He stands by ready to give His fruits of patience and longanimity.

GOODNESS: As followers of Jesus we are expected to love our neighbor who is kind to us, or at least does us no harm We are mandated by Jesus to love those close to us and even those ready to do us harm or who have already harmed us. You and I both know that the first is easy enough but the second takes all of the spiritual strength we can muster. Jesus makes it pretty clear: "A new command I give you: Love one another, as I have loved you, so you must love one another."(John 13:34) In looking at those who cross our paths during life, we are asked not to look at them through our own eyes but through the eyes of Jesus. We know full well that He did not give a command which He Himself did not obey. Nor did He simply have some sort of an affection for friends and foes. He went forth in action, allowing Himself to be humiliated, scourged and crucified. He is saying that our love, even for our enemies, is to be expressed in action. St. John, the beloved Apostle, says that "it is not enough just to wish to do what is good, it is necessary actually to do it." (1 John 3:18)

The fruit of goodness is like a balm that fills the soul making it easy to follow through on these commands of love. The soul is saturated with goodness and whoever it encounters experiences some effects from it. It is close to the beatitude of "Blessed are the meek for they will inherit the earth." The world takes advantage of the meek. It considers them pushovers, easy to take advantage of. Inheriting of the earth has to be taken spiritually. Meek people attract those of good-will and are able to be of help to them. If the meek suffer at the hands of the evil, justice will be meted out, but in God's time and in His way. Those who have goodness as one of the qual-ities that they are known by, are very often taken advantage of. This should be of no surprise. That is the way they treated Jesus. The Holy Spirit, with His fruit of goodness makes it easy for the person, even when suffering, to share the joy of good-ness with others.

BENIGNITY: Goodness gives assistance to the soul to wish well of others and to do what is good for them. To wish well to all is not enough to obey the commandment as stated previ-ously. As St. John said, one must actually extend himself to do some good thing. Surely no one can help all people in need. It is the Holy Spirit, with this particular fruit of benignity, Who orders our actual good deeds. It is this fruit of His that puts some regularity into it. The Holy Spirit has fruits that cover every facet of life. The two fruits of goodness and benignity deal with others directly. The former five give some special character to the receiving soul. It is incumbent upon the followers of Jesus not only to have a love relationship with Him but one must reach out to others. We have been created as individuals and also as members of society. Even hermits and cloistered religious are bound, after arriving to a fullness of love for Christ, to reach out and to share the goodness that flows out of that relationship with others.

MILDNESS: An expression of goodness is mildness. The goodness in one does not wish to direct anger at anyone. If anger is directed on itself, the soul returns kindness. The world knows another way. It has reverted to the eye for an eye prin-ciple of the Old Testament. Jesus insists that we turn the other cheek. It is not weakness. It is strength to be meek and mild. It is not goodness by withdrawal, it is goodness by a forward, loving thrust. Jesus gives us this direction. He says, "Take my yoke upon you and learn from me, for I am meek and humble of heart, and you will find rest for your souls." (Matt. 11:29)

FAITH: You have met faith in your reading but not this one. This is the fruit of faith as bestowed by the Spirit, to give assistance to the soul to be LOYAL. Loyalty does come as a result of believing in someone on the natural and on the supernatural level. As one believes in God with vibrance enough to offer one's life, there comes the quality of loyalty. One is to be loyal to Jesus not only as one is to a King but also as one is to a Friend. The Holy Spirit has done, and continues to do, so much for the soul by way of this extra impetus to believing in Jesus and following in His Footsteps, that the soul gives Jesus the loyalty of faithfulness. It can be and often is, a loyalty unto death. "No one has greater love than this, to lay down one's life for one's friends." (John 15:13)

MODESTY: From our present day understanding, modesty means dressing, looking and walking properly. It mostly seems to be used with regard to clothes and bodily postures that these not be a source of temptations of a sexual nature to others. As it was used in the time of St. Paul, it had reference mostly to moderation. Everything was to be done in moderation; not too much, not too little. It is still a quality that asks for prudence in the use of all things; things of the body, and things of the soul.

The fruit of modesty helps the soul not to become enslaved to creatures. In the beginning, everything in nature was ordered. As a result of sin, the order of things vanished. Christ came to give order to all things again. Everything is to be done with justice and charity. Freedom from sin and enslavements are what His Teachings and His Life introduced to fallen man. Riches, power, and lusts are what enslave the soul. The fruit of modesty is given to the soul to make it easier to order all creatures in a way that would not hold it back from achieving its goal but, instead, be a help to it on its way there.

CONTINENCE: This has direct reference to disorder in the use of sex. Sex was made by God to be beautiful. It is to be an integral part of love making when those who have been bonded together in marriage have the right to express it with their whole being, body and soul; a total giving of each to the other. The world has introduced a selfish aspect to this, wherein each uses the other for self-gratification, rather than for a selfless gift to the other. To make love is the ideal; to have sex is the profanation. Continence is the proper use of the sex faculty in accordance with God's design. The fruit is given by the Spirit to make this ordering easier, in fact, to make it a joy. To those who don't know any better, every deprivation in the use of this faculty would seem like enslavement. The opposite is true. To drive between the guard rails on the highway might seem to be confining but, in fact, they extend to the driver the liberty of getting to his destination in safety. The sex factor of life is real and has to be dealt with. For those outside of the marital bond, it is sinful to give in to sexual expressions. The fruit of continence permeates the soul so that it does not become snarled on its journey toward a total and free love union with God.

CHASTITY: Chastity, as a fruit, is different from chastity as a virtue. It is meant to be a help to the soul. It means that the person is not enslaved by sexual forces but that one is in charge with ease and with joy. There is a proper chastity to be observed certainly by those who are single but also by those who are married. There is a purity that is to enter even into the use of sex by those bonded in marital love.

In conclusion, there is something that must be assumed when speaking of the fruits of the Holy Spirit. When there is a life of intimacy with the Spirit, virtue abounds in all areas and in addition to a holy life, the soul becomes confirmed in grace which makes it easier for it to deal lovingly with itself, with other humans, and with all creatures. It is what could be looked upon as a romantic life with the Spirit, wherein there is joy in performing those things that Jesus expects. They are not carried out with a sense of obligation, but with a sense of loyalty to a Friend. The bond between the soul and its God, whether it is with the Father, with Jesus, or with the Holy Spirit, is indeed a love bond. The soul, saturated in love, serves the Individual Members of the Trinity in a filial manner and at the same time allows itself to enjoy basking in Their loving embrace. It finds itself, so to speak, as an incorporated individual, living in unity with the Three Persons to carry out Their wishes with ease and joy. It receives Their expressions of love freely and concerns itself with the work of saving souls, thus bringing glory in a manner to that is unique to Each Member of the Trinity.

CHAPTER 25

Your Heart and
Your Spiritual Cholesterol I

*"You stiff-necked people
uncircumcised in hearts and ears!
You always oppose the Holy Spirit;
you are just like your ancestors."*
(Acts 7:51)

*C*holesterol is a term health-conscious people the world over know well. It represents a condition in which the blood flow to and from the heart is hampered due to the buildup of a certain substance on the inner walls of the arteries. Because of this, the heart must work harder to keep enough blood flowing to the brain. Physical damages have been the result of this condition. Spiritual cholesterol is a parallel to the physical condition wherein the flow of graces and the gifts of the Holy Spirit are impeded due to qualities found within a soul that resist the generosity of the Holy Spirit. For a healthy spiritual life, there is a need to clear up this resistance to allow the Spirit free access to the soul for its additional spiritual enrichment.

There are a number of conditions in the physical and spiritual makeup of each individual that prevent a closer relationship with God. Some of these blockages are of a moral nature involving sin. Others are of a physical or psychological nature that do not involve moral consequences. The first category involves the seven Capital Sins. It is these that will take up our interest in this chapter. It is not within the scope of this treatise to explore this area in an extensive way as in moral theology but briefly and to the point that you, dear reader, might at least have a glimpse of something that can be worked on in the future. The purpose of the presentation here is to make you aware of those elements in spiritual life which may cause you to wonder why it is that the Holy Spirit is not doing more for you. You and I both realize that He is very generous. If you do not experience this generosity, you might find that in the total list of blockages a certain number of them might be the culprits. To clear them up through prayer, and perhaps some spiritual direction, will no doubt result in a deeper peace and a greater joy. The blockages in the order that they will be treated are as follows: Pride, Anger, Sloth, Envy, Covetousness, Avarice, and Lust.

PRIDE: Pride is on top of the list due to the large amount of damage it does to the spiritual life of the greatest number of people. It first entered into God's presence by one of His greatest creations, Lucifer. As one of the most gifted angels before the throne of God he became impressed with himself. He chose not to give due recognition to God and thus was cast out of God's presence. Adam and Eve, tricked by the fallen Lucifer, followed suit. At his prompting, they took their glance from God, and directed onto themselves. They fell into pride by preferring themselves to God. They chose to go the way of Lucifer rather than the way pointed out for them by God. This stigma remains to this day in all of their children.

Pride is a denial of dependence on God as the source of one's life. It is a failure to give due recognition to the Maker for the good that He has done and the Person Who He is. One's glance is taken away from Him and put onto one's self. It is the continuous gaze on one's self that causes one to disregard and even ignore God and to live as if God did not even exist.

When one is filled with himself there is no room for God. Everything pivots around the self. One's ego becomes so swollen that one cannot see beyond it. Everyone else is put on a lower level. Jesus gives us this example:

"Two men went up to the temple to pray, one a Pharisee and the other a tax collector. The Pharisee took up his position and spoke this prayer of himself, 'O God, I thank you that I am not like the rest of men, — greedy, dishonest, adulterous — or even like this tax collector. I fast twice a week, and I pay tithes on my whole income.' But the tax collector stood off at a distance and would not even raise his eyes to heaven but beat his breast and prayed, 'O God, be merciful to me a sinner.' I tell you, the latter went home justified, not the former; for everyone who exults himself will be humbled and the one who humbles himself will be exalted." (Luke 18:9-14)

All of God's children are to be as brothers and sisters. Each one is to look up to the other, and not down as did the Pharisee.

Pride is an abomination to God. It is detestable because it is living a lie. Pride is blind and sees no one other than one's self.

No one else counts for anything. The world is full of it. Satan and his legions of devils roam throughout the world tainting it with their pride. You and I are caught in the grips of it. It can cling to us without our knowing it. As disciples of Jesus we are called to humility. From His Own Words He makes this known to us:"Take My yoke upon you and learn from Me, for I am gentle and humble in heart, and you will find rest for your souls." (Matt. 11:29)

It is this humble spirit, when there is an acknowledgment in actual life that each one of us depends on God for every single breath, that is pleasing to the Holy Spirit. Humility gives Him space. It cleanses all the resistance to His generosity. With the acceptance of the truth of totally belonging to God, the hardness of the heart vanishes. The heart becomes docile and pliable so that He can form it, inflame it, energize it, and sanctify it.

ANGER: Anger is a passion that is fired up because of pride. If one does not have his/her way, anger is a force that could do physical and spiritual harm toward the one against whom it is directed. It could lead to many other evils like revenge, stealing, murder. Anger in itself is not a pure evil as is pride. There is a justifiable anger as demonstrated by Jesus in cleansing the temple of the buyers and sellers who desecrated His Father's House. Since pride is at the seat of anger, one becomes blind, loses control and hardly knows what she/he is doing. It is this loss of control that makes anger such an evil. Its consequences have no bounds on those who are its victims.

What anger does to an individual crippled by it is that it completely eliminates any possible intervention on the part of the Holy Spirit. The spiritual arteries are completely blocked. No grace can pass through. Anger not only does damage to others, it does damage to one's self by depriving one of any possible help, any possible healing, and any possible grace. The Holy Spirit has this to say about anger through the Scriptures: "My dear brothers, take note of this: Everyone should be quick to listen, slow to speak and slow to become angry, for man's anger does not bring about the righteous life that God desires." (James 1:19-20) Often small irritations build up. One should practice diffusing anger before it gets out of hand. Instead of holding things in, when possible, they should be brought out. If anger is returned with anger, the initial anger is intensified. Jesus' directive of turning the other cheek is not popular in the world today. That is why murders beget murders and wars beget wars. Jesus told Peter in the Garden of Gethsemane that whoever lives by the sword will die by the sword. Anger expressed in a damaging way exposes one's lack of discipline over his/her temper. The sad thing about this sin is that there is no lasting help unless it comes from above. Here is one case in which many persons are their own worst enemy. An habitually angry person cuts his own throat, so to speak, since he cuts off the possibility of help from the Holy Spirit Who would be only too willing to give it.

SLOTH: Sloth is a state of the body and soul in which there is no energy to do anything. This condition should not be confused with a state of physical, psychological, emotional, or spiritual disability. When an individual becomes incapacitated through no fault of its own, that state would not constitute sloth. There is guilt connected with sloth. A person could be active but chooses not to. Personally, I am very careful in making any judgements concerning a person who is not doing what one should. There are many causes in our day that contribute to damaging the human person for which the person has no, or very little responsibility. We live in an environment wherein there is an intensified and accelerated attack on the human race in general by the evil one and his company. Satan has entered in to control the way of life in the twentieth century in such a thorough way that he effects its entire moral culture. He has worked cleverly and with evil intent to destroy the willpower of humans. He is the master who knows well how to enervate a will so that it cannot function even in the fulfillment of ordinary duties. We must think twice before putting individuals into the category of sin. Prayer would be the best solution to be taken up for those who are so afflicted. This would open the door for the Holy Spirit to offer custom made solutions for those needing help in this area.

Sloth, as a sinful condition, would be caused when, for example, an individual seeks out the comfortable and pleasurable life to avoid having to work toward goodness. Usually a person who draws away from all responsibility knows that he or she is guilty. Within one's conscience, there is a knowledge that convicts a person when he or she knows that a certain way of life in not in accord with God's wishes. Such a person chooses the carefree life in order to dodge having to take responsibility for his/her actions.

There is a serious condition requiring a warning. It is in the area of the Faithful in which there is a habitual seeking what is new in the apparition, locution, message, department instead of making an effort to implement that which is already known. It is much easier to go looking for new information than to buckle down and become involved in carrying out what has already been presented. It amounts to a chronic curiosity. On the other hand, the Faithful who keep hearing of the happenings in Medjugorje and other places where private revelations are allegedly taking place should be made aware that Jesus chided the apostles and disciples for not recognizing the signs of the times. Fluffing it off casually as nonsense can also be sloth-flavored. Others who should also heed a warning are they who run after the newest spiritual book just to feed their insatiable mind. Finally, there is the reader of the Bible who reads and reads and does not stop to take in what has been read. There is a certain pleasure that the mind seeks for in what is novel. When one is hooked on this pursuit of pleasure, whether it be by an incessant reading of the Scriptures or other spiritual works, there can be a guilt in the realm of spiritual gluttony.

I wish to come to the defense of those who have been damaged by the atmosphere of the latter part of our century when it comes to the inability of the human will to function properly. In my ministry I have conducted will workshops to help remedy the condition. These have proven most helpful. Just as a ball of twine can become tangled up, it is my conviction that this is exactly what Satan has been doing full time in the present generation. The workshops have assisted many to become unsnarled so that they can come back into a life of normal activity with hope. My personal plea to the Lord is to have mercy on our generation for the fact that it is being hit below the belt by an essentially evil force — Satan and the world milieu that he has created to snag souls on their journey toward salvation.

ENVY: Envy can be defined as the sadness within a person over the good fortune that befalls another. This condition would be somewhat rooted in pride in that God has not blessed you as much as He has blessed others. There is usually a lack of appreciation of one's own blessings. Looking out to see what others are doing and you are not, and what others have and you don't, may cause you to be so preoccupied with the blessings of others that you are not aware of the blessings that God has given you. Holy Job mentions envy in his remark that "resentment kills a fool, envy slays the simple." Envy truly has a devastating effect on one's heart.

The human soul is always craving deeper fulfillment. This is because God created the soul for Himself and it continues to be unsatiated even if it crams into itself all sorts of satisfactions. It is not quantity that the soul seeks. It looks for quality. No amount of finites can satisfy a soul that was created to seek after the Infinite God.

Stop dead in your tracks if you should be tempted to envy. Take a moment to count your own blessings. Pray that you become satisfied with whatever the Lord has given to you. Gratitude to God for His generosity in your own life is a good antidote to cast off the very wretched feelings that come with envy.

COVETOUSNESS: This sin goes beyond envy. Envy looks at the good fortunes of others and becomes saddened by them.

Covetousness looks at the goods that others have and causes one to want them so passionately that one is ready to do harm in order to attain them. The last two commandments deal with the coveting of one's neighbor's wife and goods. Be reminded that the reason why this sin is called capital is because other sins can flow from it. Coveting has caused people to go out to steal, murder, and commit adultery. Such internal cravings truly plug up the flow of the influence that the Holy Spirit can have on a soul.

God have mercy on the people of our day. All hell has broken loose, and with the use of the media and, the entertainment world in general, the eyes of the people of our day are ready to pop out when they see all the things presented to them and are not obtainable. Every time an advertisement is presented in living color on TV, it causes dissatisfaction to be experienced on the part of viewers if they are not able to afford what is being offered. The Lord has warned that one cannot serve God and money. What are all the advertisements about? Money, money, and more money for those who are offering these things.

The beautiful quality of sex created by God for the filling of heaven with human beings, is being exploited once again by those who are money hungry. With cable TV, the satellite dish, pay-for-view, any gratification of sex can be had in the privacy of one's home. Do you think that electricity was invented by God? One may begin to wonder.

To stay clear of the dreadful internal inclination of covetousness, learn to have power over your eyes and ears. If you were to enter a home where the smell of escaping gas or putrid garbage hits your nose, you would certainly cover your nose. This should be done with what comes into your home. Love yourself enough to ward off these accessible troublemakers. The journey to heaven is difficult enough without putting traps in your own path.

AVARICE: In a way this has been mentioned briefly above. As grace begets grace, one evil begets another. When offered all the exceptional goodies in life for the price of a few or more dollars, who can help but to crave money. Money is presented as the solution to all troubles. If you have enough money, you can get anything that is offered by any one of the many professions and commodity markets of the world.

If one has money, it never seems to be enough to buy the new things that become available each month. Those who look continuously at the size of their bank account, look for deposits to be made so that more interest can be gained, so that more property can be bought or stocks obtained, so as to get more money for more interest and on and on it goes. When Jesus mentioned to his disciples that it is easier for a camel to go through the eye of a needle than for a rich man to enter into heaven, they gasped. "Then who can be saved?" They knew by their own experience that everyone wants money. It is a need. Without being satisfied by the infinite, the heart will never be happy. Jesus tells us: "What does it profit a man if he gains the whole world and suffers the loss of his soul in the process?"

Maybe now you can better appreciate the chapter on detachment. In one of the Masses in honor of holy men and women, the statement comes up, "They could have sinned, but did not." That same statement should be before your eyes to deal with the evils of today. Beg the Holy Spirit frequently to assist you to get rid of anything in your heart that would block even the smallest bit of grace. Ask Him even to remind you to ask Him for help. It is impossible to be saved without grace. You should direct your strongest energies to obtain and retain clean spiritual arteries.

LUST: We have touched on this subject in a small way above. It is the inordinate craving for sexual excitement especially brought in through the eyes. Jesus knew about it because it was around in His day. He said: "But I tell you that anyone who looks at a woman lustfully has already committed adultery with her in his heart." (Matt. 5:28) He refined the law concerning adultery so that it included the cravings for sex

pleasure. Seeing what has happened through technology and the easy availability of pornography to habitually gratify the sexual passions one can only beg God on his knees to be preserved in the virtue of purity. With human efforts alone, it
5 has become impossible. The Lord says, however, "with God all things are possible." As with the other capital sin, lust, too, comes from pride and it can flow into multiple avenues of sin.

Unless you are dead serious and you really and truly want to save your soul, you will not escape the lures that are set before
10 you. Let me re-emphasize, you need to have a strong will to protect yourself from occasions of sin. You have to be tough in spirit to make it through all the traps set for you. You cannot allow your gazes to go just anywhere. Out of love for yourself choose to keep a strong desire within your heart to remain
15 pure. Latch onto the Holy Spirit as a young child clutches to its mother in a terrifying situation. Reach out to Him as a drowning person reaches out for a life preserver. I would suggest, before going on with more reading that you rest for a few minutes and come to internal silence and peace so that
20 the Spirit can refuel your soul for yet another segment of your journey.

CHAPTER 26

Your Heart and
Your Spiritual Cholesterol II

> *"Go up to a land flowing with milk
> and honey. But I myself will not go up
> in your company, because you are a
> stiff-necked people; otherwise I might
> exterminate you on the way."*
>
> *(Exod. 33:3)*

*I*n the previous chapter, specific blockages to the flow of God's grace were considered. These had a moral consequence attached to them. A person in guilt not only sins by a rebelliousness against God, but harms his soul with an obstruction through which the Holy Spirit may not pass into the soul to give it the gifts that are ascribed to that soul through Baptism. In this chapter, we will give attention to particular blockages that basically are not of a sinful nature but that, nonetheless, prevent a flow of the gifts of the Holy Spirit from doing good for the soul with the blockage. Any individual may have one or more of the following blockages and so it more difficult for the Holy Spirit to do His Work. We will consider specific blockages in this chapter, and a few more in the next.

The distinct blockages that will be covered in this chapter are as follows: Fear, Self-Consciousness, Low-Self Image, Self-Pity, Tiredness, and Routine. It will not be possible to give these an exhaustive treatment but enough so that you can identify them within yourself and do something about increasing the flow of the gifts of the Holy Spirit into your soul.

FEAR: A little fear is good for the soul's sake but, when it goes over a certain point, it can be a hindrance rather than a help. It is my professional belief that there are more souls crippled by fear than ordinarily one would suspect. Usually it starts in childhood. Those who are responsible for forming the young soul may not realize that the nervous and emotional systems of the young infant and the little child are very sensitive. Any traumatic experience could damage a person for life unless dealt with properly, or unless that person is blessed by being able in time to tap into the healing power of the Holy Spirit. The more conscious a person is of his or her fears and the more attention one gives to them, the more the fears grow and the more damaging they are to the soul. Parents and grandparents, and all who have the care of little ones, should be alerted to the need to always deal with their little charges in a kindly, tender, and loving manner as Jesus did. If parents and others who care for the little ones are themselves crippled by an excessive fear, that fear is transmitted to the children.

When the elders around a little child excessively use the words, such as "Watch out! Don't touch that! NO! The bogey man will get you! You will go to hell!" these phrases can cause them to lose their inner peace. The word, NO, should be used sparingly. It is better to say things like, "No, you may not do that but you may do this," or, "No, you may not play with that but you may play with this." If little ones are bit by bit squeezed into a corner with hardly any "YESES," their fear level will intensify.

If you should find yourself in a higher level of fear than you know is good for you, prayer to the Holy Spirit, Jesus, and Mary would be helpful. Imagining yourself as a little child and allowing yourself to climb up on Jesus' or Mary's lap to be cuddled by them, will be of great benefit. It is not a bad idea, even if you are forty, and fifty, and more, to do just that. How soothing is the statement, "But Jesus, I'm only a little girl/boy," or "I can't possibly do all that everyone wants me to," etc. How often has Jesus advised, "Be not afraid." Pope John Paul II wrote an entire book on that theme. How helpful it would be especially for the young in your social circle, were you to take on a personal little ministry of allaying unnecessary fears in their hearts.

In my own life, if I did not have the mother that I had, I would not be here. First, for obvious reasons, secondly she trained all thirteen of us not to be afraid. She encouraged us to try things that we never did before. If we hesitated, she would say, "Oh, come on, you can do that. God will help you. Try it." If we still were cautious, she would go right along to prove to us that we could do it… and we did. She would be very stern with the older kids who for any reason put fear into the young ones.

So, dear reader, don't be afraid even of fear. Prayer, good, but, hearty prayer is the source of greater help. As you turn to the Holy Spirit, He will send you to Mary, and Mary may send you to Jesus, and behold, little by little, even if you have been deadly afraid for years and years, they have the power to heal you right on the spot. Believe me. Try it and go into a trusting stance. All sorts of therapies are offered by those who are trained in this area, however, do remember that Jesus and the Holy Spirit are the Top Experts.

SELF-CONSCIOUSNESS: This too is a big one. This too is triggered in early childhood. The child in its early years is not self-conscious by nature. It may explore its nose and its toes but it has no self-reflection because the instrument of self-reflection has not yet been developed. If God had designed it to be, the child would have become stunted in its emotional and spiritual growth. Adults should take care not to make issues for a child that could make it self-conscious for years to come. Telling a child over and over things like "Don't you have a pretty dimple," or "Look how dumb you are," or "You have such a big nose," can undermine the child's self-esteem, make it self-conscious, and inhibit its personal development.

As adults we do ourselves and the Holy Spirit a disservice if whenever we do something, half of our attention is on what we are doing and the other half is on watching ourselves as we do it. It may be that we are deathly afraid of making a mistake, or we are bent on pleasing people, or we have been trained to mistrust our actions. All of these tend to make us habitually self-conscious.

Should you find yourself as an adult to be plagued by an excessive amount of self-consciousness it may be advantageous for you to seek help, or to take up the re-training yourself. It would take effort and patience, but it could be done. One possible danger here is that you could get right into the trap of watching yourself to see if you are watching yourself. Your second condition would be worse than the first. You may want to put yourself into the presence of your Guardian Angel and let him watch you. He would be very gentle with you and, without being critical, would advise you on either how to do something better or tell you that you are doing a good job.

It goes without saying that you should never watch the Holy Spirit to see what He is doing within your soul. If you do He will stop because you are giving Him the message that you don't trust Him. Trust Him and let Him do what His Wisdom and Love direct Him to do. You will always be blessed more by Him if you give Him all the space that He needs.

LOW SELF-IMAGE: This is a common blockage. It too could have crept in somewhere as one grows up. What it does to obstruct the work of the Holy Spirit is to keep a continuous tape running in one's mind such as, "He'll never bless YOU. He'll never give YOU gifts." A person whose healthy self-image has been struck down has lost confidence. That individual believes he or she can't ever do anything right and is too stupid, too awkward, too slow, too ugly, too fat, too skinny, too this or too that. The individual has no confidence. They think that it is normal for everyone around them to find fault with what they do. Parents should be warned. Statements like, "Why aren't you like your sister…?" "We wanted a boy and look what we got, a GIRL…". Degrading statements when the young people are so sensitive can be crippling. "I love you as you are for WHO you are," is a good thing to say. Uplifting remarks will do well for the young person. There is no need to go overboard, but a compliment or a pat on the back will go a long way to assure a healthy self-image. A child needs to help to build up a healthy confidence. One particularly sobering truth for parents to keep in heart is this one: God gave you that child to help it to flower into a beautiful person. That child is HIS. He has put the child into your hands so that you would cooperate with Him to bring it to a full stature in body and soul. It is not easy to raise children in this our day. Nonetheless, the responsibility remains. Help from above is as close as a sincere prayer.

You might want to reread the chapter on dignity, dear heart, if you have problems with a low self-image. There is no need to have to live with this impediment to grace. Remember, you are special to God. You are unique. There is no one like you in all the world. You are invited to have a good and healthy self-respect. Do not be afraid that you will slip into pride. Just remember that what you have is from God. God does not make junk. God loves you and respects you. The Holy Spirit is a frequent Healer of this sort of malady. You might want to go to Him to put yourself into His care and trustingly allow Him to work on your low self-image. His may be painful but it will be rewarding. A one-liner that would be beneficial is this one, "God loves me, I love me, if YOU don't love me, it's YOUR problem!" It also goes back to what has been said previously. One with this malady could gain self-respect by remembering the difference between the WHO and the WHATS. As a WHO every human being has a dignity before God. What God thinks of you must become more important to you than what people think of you, and even more important than what you think of yourself. His estimation of you is always right; not so the estimation that either you have of yourself or people have of you.

SELF-PITY: It is easy to slip into "WOE is me. POOR me. No one has the problems I have," or "No one is sick like I am." Well, of course, I think that you may already smell the pride in remarks like that. When a person who is self-centered, sees only his/her own condition, it is not difficult to slip into this condition. Sympathy is something that we all enjoy. A little bit of it goes a long way. If people don't give you a drop or two, and you have to give it to ourselves, it's OK, but be easy with it. It could become harmful if you become emotionally dependent on it. It is then when it becomes a barrier to grace. One can become so filled with self that there is no room for the Holy Spirit.

If you have it tough, He is the One you go to. One needs a plunge from self into the loving Person of the Holy Spirit. One immersed in self pity needs to give one's self as a gift to the Holy Spirit. The Spirit readily accepts that gift of self and in exchange enlivens His gifts within that soul causing self pity gradually to fade away.

There are times when this self-pity is never verbalized and keeps nagging at one's insides. This is an even worse condition. A good and healthy prayer life is once again the best real solution. The Lord will give you sympathy. He might just say to you, "What are you complaining about? Look at what I went through. Compared to the sufferings of Jesus, and compared to the sufferings of other people, you may not have it too bad. All one has to do, if they are stuck in the mud with self-pity, is to walk the corridors of a hospital. No matter what you are suffering whether you yourself are in a hospital or outside of it, you will always find someone who is in a far worse condition that you are. Once you leave yourself and have compassion for another, your self-pity will subside.

Self-pity becomes concretized in a person if and when he or she falls into the habit of comparing one's condition with that of other people. If a person would put his or her nose to the grindstone and concentrate on what it is that they should be doing in life, the self-pity, would shrivel up from lack of attention and blow away. When concentration is put on any deficiency it makes that deficiency hang around more and even get worse. Every individual put upon this earth by God has goodness in them. Were one to put his or her mind on that goodness, self-pity would soon disappear.

As in any difficulty, the best answer is good solid prayer. When I say that, I do not mean SAY prayers, I mean pray from the heart. The Lord does tell us that if we ask, we will receive. The Holy Spirit is right within us, at our beck and call. If He is not made use of, one has only to blame one's self. If healing is at the door and no effort is made to accept it, then one deserves to wallow in self-pity. There are those who get hooked on self-pity. They would not know how to behave without it. Self-pity is a burden on the individual as well as the people who have to live with someone hardened in it. If you have to pity yourself, do it once a day with different people and keep track of them to be able to make the rounds once a month.

TIREDNESS: One might wonder how tiredness would effect the generosity of the Holy Spirit. Tiredness brings down the level of human behavior. Tiredness slows down the operation of the mind and makes the will respond with a low level of enthusiasm. Hardly any verbal explanation needs to be given because everyone who has ever been tired knows its effects on every level of human activity. It obviously lowers the grade of one's prayer and tends to be a cause of giving it up completely. Tiredness regulates the flow of grace into a soul more than is suspected. When overtired, people don't realize how their human performance has deteriorated. At times mothers and fathers and many others who are dedicated, work, and work, and work, without taking proper rest or needed recreation. I remember when I was in charge of a hermitage, Sisters would come to the Hermitage for their annual retreat after school closed down for the summer. It was the Holy Spirit Himself Who came to their rescue when He made me address them in this fashion, "Sister, you may not begin your retreat until you rest. Sleep as long as you need and then your retreat will start." Do you know that some of those Sisters slept for thirty-six hours straight? They did not even know how tired they were. Mothers too, especially with two or three toddlers in their care go on and on and on. The helpful advice on my part is that they take a nap in the afternoon along with the little ones, so that when the others come home from school, and Dad gets in from work, Mom, with her second wind, can handle things much better. Mothers in the work force, coming home to take on the family needs, are still another group who require considerable rest.

Do not underestimate the wall that tiredness puts up against the generosity of the Holy Spirit. Tiredness comes on so gradually that one hardly is aware that his or her performance level in all areas of life has fallen. In obeying the commandment that we are to love God with our whole being, soul, mind, and heart, the Lord may be cheated if the human system is almost washed out with tiredness. When tiredness sets in, it is impossible to give to the Lord in worship and service all that He deserves.

What is the solution? Rest, naturally. It should be a genuine rest. It should not be a rest made up of cat-naps. A tense and rigid body is a good indication that proper and sufficient rest is lacking. If you find that you have to push yourself to do what is expected of you, the energy used in that pushing tires you out all the more. The thing to do is to sit down or lie down and refuse to do anything until you find a deliberateness within you. If you have no will to do something, don't do it. Give yourself a bit of time to find your will (heart). If you cannot put your whole heart into some particular activity that you are being called to do, postpone doing it until you find your heart even if it takes a week. Yeah, but... . I know, I know. However, the Lord does not want forced service. If your heart is not in it, the work does not compute in heaven. Better for you to do less with heart, than much without it. One of the things that makes most people more tired than they like to admit is the runaway mind. If you find this to be the case with you, turn off your mind, take a good nap, and then get back with it. Even Jesus recognized all of this. In the Scriptures, we read, "Then because so many people were coming and going that they did not even have a chance to eat, He said to them, 'Come away by yourselves to a deserted place and rest a while.'" (Mark 6:31) And again He says, "Come to me, all you who labor and are burdened and I will give you rest." (Matt. 11:28) Jesus had a tremendous responsibility to save souls. He was on fire with wanting to get to as many towns as possible, but He still took time to rest. A powerful lesson!

ROUTINE: Too much routine in your life can make you feel like a robot. Our age is so machine oriented that those who work with machines tend to become somewhat like them. It should be a matter of dignity to refuse to do anything unless you do it as a full-fledged human being with clear mind and free will. Anything else is degrading and beneath the dignity that the Loving Creator bestowed upon us. A good rule of thumb is to cease and desist in undertaking anything that would make you feel less human. I know that it will take time and you will slow down at first, but you will not change from being a robot until you stamp your foot on the floor, pound your fist on the table and say, "I am a HUMAN BEING, I am NOT a machine." Say this to yourself first for a dry run. When you know that you mean it, then try it in public. "Yes, but how about my job. I may get fired." If you had been a good machine and you convince your boss that, as a human being, you will do even better, your job will be secure. If you are a mother, and you have to pull this on your family, tape a sign on the refrigerator door such as, "THIS week is now being declared a 'do your own laundry week.' Mother is NOT a robot!"

Once in awhile, just break routine for the sake of breaking it. If you always do something the same way, dare to change and do it a bit differently. If you always take the same road to work or to church, once in awhile choose the more scenic route. If you want a good challenge, listen to your speech. Are you one who says, ah-h-h-h-h after every sentence? Make an effort. Become aware of it and cut it out. No need to use it as a connecter. If you need to think what you are going to say next, stop (dead silence) and then say it without the introduction of the, ah-h-h-h-h. The other common one is, "you know ..." If you find that every fourth word is a "you know," break the routine. Become fresh and deliberate in all that you say.

The Holy Spirit will be delighted if you become totally human to Him. In this way, He will be able to become totally Divine to you, and you will be the one to gain. You might want to take a little rest now. There are more blockages I wish to share with you, but enough for now. We'll take on a few more in the next chapter.

CHAPTER 27

Your Heart and
Your Spiritual Cholesterol III

*"And he said, 'if I have found favor in
Thy sight, O Lord, let the Lord , I pray
Thee, go in the midst of us, although
it is a stiff-necked people; and pardon
our iniquity and our sin, and take us
for Thy inheritance.'"*

(Exod. 34:9)

D id you ever wonder why there is so much confusion and so little reverence in so many of the parish churches? As I travel the country, I am exposed to it and it is heartbreaking. Our Lord told us that the Church will last till the end of time, and this will be so. There are those who in our day have vowed to destroy it. They are working hard at it on various levels. The real reason for all of this is that the Holy Spirit is being sabotaged from doing His work among the faithful and among the clergy as well. The only and the best answer is to remove every bit of spiritual cholesterol.

In the Upper Room there was no resistance whatever. On the contrary, there was an energetic readiness for His coming. OK, it's understandable because of the circumstances. However, from this it is clear that the power and effectiveness of the Holy Spirit depends on the disposition of the faithful to receive Him and to benefit from His generosity. The positive answer to the above question is that in too many of the faithful, there are blockages to grace. The working solution is not to point fingers at what others are or are not doing. Rather, I must make sure that I do not contribute to the confusion or the lessening of reverence. It is for me to make sure MY spiritual arteries are clean, so that the Holy Spirit can work in ME, through ME, and with ME, for the sake of the entire parish community.

In the last chapter we learned of six distinct blockages. In this chapter, we will take up six more. These are: Procrastination, Easy Living, Distressed Mind, Uncontrollable Cravings, Noise, and Business. Again, these subjects will not be dealt with in depth. However, if you become aware of their existence within your own soul, you will be able to check in with the Holy Spirit and, with His help, you will be able to identify your personal hindrances to a more perfect life.

PROCRASTINATION: At last you have a ringside seat to watch at close range the conflict that goes on between the head and the heart. Procrastination is the proof of the pudding as to which of these two faculties of the soul is to be given preeminence. To procrastinate means to put off. The head understands that something is to be done. The word gets to the heart. Will the heart follow through on the report of the head or will it balk? The head keeps on pestering that the deadline is getting close. There is still no response. At the hour when the task is to be completed, the head screams to the heart, "Get going." Finally, because the heart is reminded by the head that if the task is not completed within the hour, there will be a fine to pay of one hundred and fifty dollars. So, the heart gets its act together and finally, finally, at the very last moment, the task is completed and peace reigns between the head and the heart once more. The point of the matter is: the head can have all of the knowledge it wants. If the heart is not going to follow through on the knowledge, the knowledge remains sterile and nonproductive.

The slovenly heart is the cause of much grief on every level of life. It is especially detected and agonized over in family living. The electric bill arrives. The wife puts it on her husband's desk in the den and tells him where it is. Days turn into weeks. She asks if he had paid it. "No," he answers, "I'll take care of it tomorrow." Tomorrow comes and goes and still the bill is not paid. Circumstances arise and he must go out of town on business. As he is leaving for the airport, she hands him the electric bill. It is five weeks overdue. He takes it with him, and as he goes out the door, his last words are, "I'll put it into my briefcase and send it out when I get to San Francisco." He gets entangled with business the minute he arrives at the airport. He stays two weeks, and completes the job. On the way home he discovers the bill in the briefcase as he sits back to relax on his return flight. He arrives home. It's late, and everyone is asleep. It's all dark. He turns on the hallway switch to make his way upstairs to the bedroom. The switch must be broken; nothing happened when he turned it on. Well, to make a long story short, the electricity was turned off. The family was without it for four days. That is a typical example, a little farfetched, but one that happens over and over again in one form or another.

For many, procrastination is such a fixed behavior pattern that people learn to live with the procrastinator. This type of putting off things to be done also hits the spiritual life. Putting off reconciliation, putting off praying, putting off reading the Scripture, putting off joining a prayer group, putting off on following through on Mary's messages, putting off on becoming serious, putting off taking Jesus at His Word, putting off getting to Mass on time. On and on it goes. Such a condition is difficult for a person to change. The procrastinator procrastinates about changing his or her ways. Should the habit of procrastinating cause a very serious crisis, perhaps then, the ball of improvement may start rolling.

The procrastinator's heart is so unsettled that the Holy Spirit cannot do much. Lack of self-discipline is the chief culprit here. The will is weak. It cannot bring to itself enough power to see a task through once the head reports that it must be done. What is the solution? God's mercy and prayers by those who suffer the most from the actions of the procrastinator. A conversion could help. It would ordinarily take a bolt of lightening to bring heart and head together. Change will never come drastically. A genuine resolve to improve must come first. Grace can make this happen.

EASY LIVING: The push-button, the remote-control age, reflects the development of technology, but it has its side effects. The Western culture has changed for the worse because the spark of life has been bled out of it. It is so comfortable though. Yes, but it is also devastating. Easy living contributes to more pain than meets the eye. It especially effects the will. The will loses its elasticity, its spontaneity, its power for action, its power to change, its power to go out of its way to do something for someone in need. It creates havoc in all of the areas of life.

The easy life is highly promoted, nonetheless. It is very popular. We in the West pity the Third World nations because they are so far behind. Personally, I must take exception to that. Having traveled in these so-called "backward" countries, I found discomfort there because of my background but the people there are real people, totally human and very spiritual. They do not have what we do, but they have more of what we need. There is something about hardship that brings people together. With their lack of those things which you and I take for granted, these people are more sensitive, more compassionate, more gentle.

Be that as it may, the Holy Spirit certainly is not happy with our style of life. It has caused damage even within the Church. The Lord has told us that unless we pick up our cross and follow Him, we are not worthy of Him. Pain is part and parcel of our Christian living. Jesus did not take it easy. He came into the world when there were none of the creature comforts that you and I enjoy.

This easy life makes it a glorious time for Satan. Our hearts have become enervated to the degree that temptations are just too strong for the easy-going heart. With the lessening of our exertion, the forces of evil are having their red-letter years. The Holy Spirit would be of help if He were asked and allowed to take hold of our sickly condition. Without that, He can do nothing, for He will never force Himself on us. This is one of the reasons why Our Lady pleads for fasting and penance. It's to toughen us up for what is approaching. It reminds me of the lobster that was brought into a Chicago restaurant. The lobster was put into a huge pot. It reflected on its comfort in its new environment; nice water, a little confining, but not too bad. Someone had ordered a lobster dinner, so the fire is lighted and the temperature of the water begins to rise. "Not bad," says the lobster in delight, "Nothing so comfortable as this off the Boston Harbor." The temperature rises; the lobster winces, "What did I get myself into?" The water gets hotter. "HEY, I gotta get out of here! WHAT is going on?" The lobster tries to jump out. It can't. Its muscles have contracted and lost their strength by the heat of the water. No need to give you the end of the story. It is happening in our society, in our Church. Sad, but true.

What to do? There is nothing that can be done except to take yourself to task as I myself have already done. Don't fall for it! It's a trap! Become alert! Don't allow yourself to be lulled to sleep. That is precisely what the subversive plan of the enemy is. Weaken them, get them out of their wills, then we have them to ourselves. Enough said.

DISTRESSED MIND: The human mind is not an infinite mind. It has its limitations, it has its breaking point. Why are there so many mental hospitals? Why are so many people on all forms of medication? Why are there so many alcoholics, drug addicts, gamblers, and broken homes? The why's can go on at length. Never have we had so many colleges, universities and so many people with degrees. On the other hand, never in any other generation were there more mental institutions. There is no easy answer. Putting it into one sentence; we have never been so smart and yet so unhappy. As a young priest, I was the chaplain at an eastern state university attended by young people with the highest I.Q. levels. These were some of the smartest kids in the world. The campus was like a morgue. No real joy, but a severe need for pleasure of every flavor. There is no happiness in the mind. The youngsters were so intelligent, yet so unfulfilled.

The human mind was not created by God to know all things and to come up with all the answers. God could have given each one of us an angelic mind, but He did not. God knew what He did with the mind and why He did it. He intended for all eternity to share some of His knowledge with humans but they would have to engage their wills in order to accept His knowledge. Humankind would have to take His Word for what He said. It would have to engage the will in order to believe that what God chose to share was of a higher intelligence than the human mind could attain on its own. To rise above the ceiling of the potential of the human mind, human beings would have to become believers. They could choose not to but then they would have to accept the limitations of their power of reasoning.

That is why the mind of the modern person is so distressed. It is confined within itself. The heart has a craving for the infinite. The mind cannot produce the infinite for the will and so there is a rift between the head and the heart. It is a paradox. If the heart were left alone without the mind (because it does have a mind of its own,) it could lead the mind to God. The mind however will not allow this because then the mind would not have anything to do. At least, this is the way the mind would reason it out for itself. The natural mind always hits a ceiling. It can never go beyond itself. It could if it would lean on the heart and humble itself, to the heart, but this it will not do. Therefore, the modern mind, in its craving for fulfillment, leads its entire human system into disarray.

With such a conflict going on within the souls of humans, the Holy Spirit's "hands" are tied. He will not force Himself on the human person even if He knows that he/she is already going down for the third time. The heart cannot choose to plead for help because the mind refuses to give any recognition to the heart and the mind keeps the will so enslaved to itself that the condition of the will is hopeless. So, in the final analysis, the condition of the entire human being is hopeless. If the mind would only allow the heart to believe, it would fare better.

Is there a solution? Yes, prayer. In prayer, the mind could settle down. By the way, do you see with what wisdom Our Lady comes forward to offer the rosary? The rosary is one prayer that could calm the mind down and offer hope to the heart and through the heart to the mind. The soul could find peace through the stabilization brought on by the hearty recitation of the rosary, and the conversion process could begin. The Holy Spirit could find His way into this stabilization and through a spiritual IV injection, bring the person to his or her senses, so that the head and the heart together could benefit from the gifts of the Spirit. Four of the seven gifts are for the benefit of the mind, while three are for the benefit of the will. The entire seven gifts bring the head and the heart into a harmonious union.

UNCONTROLLABLE CRAVINGS: The world is full of incite-
ments that are mostly for the body. The presentations that are made in the media, in the newspaper, and in advertising, is all directed toward enhancing the condition of the body. Whatever is for its comfort, beauty, health, and rejuvenation, are offered in living color for all to have and enjoy. The money
people are behind it. All the needs, the cravings, the pleasures, the emotions, the passions are being exploited to satisfy the greed for money and power of a select few. You and I are prime targets. If we allow ourselves, we may be victimized by all that is being displayed. The world has its false gods. These
are: the mind and its capacity to know, the body with its senses, emotions, passions, comfort, pleasure, fun, sex, sports, money, power, and possessions. Its places of its worship are sports arenas and shopping malls. But for the grace of God, how can anyone live in the world and not become a part of it?
It offers all that is appealing to the five senses of sight, hearing, taste, smell, and touch. There is an absolute denial of the soul, God, heaven, and hell. Its greatest tragedy is death. It has conquered the limitations of pleasure. It has conquered space. It has been able to prolong life but death still stares it in
the face.

With the denial of the soul, there is the denial of the person, the will, the heart. What, then is to control the senses, the emotions, the passions? The world has no answer.

There is nothing said of self-control or discipline. This is
understandable. There is no belief in the source of control and discipline — the will. Obviously, the varied cravings of the flesh which are hitting the depths of depravity are given the oppor- tunity to be expressed without incurring guilt, without insisting on responsibility of the individual over self. That leaves the
individual with a broad spectrum of bodily expressions to explore and to enjoy without the benefit of conscience.

Where does this leave you and me? We are on our own, assisted by our conscience, our belief in God and His Commandments, by the redemption of Jesus, His Church, the Sacraments, Mother Mary, Guardian Angels, all of the souls in purgatory, all of the angels and saints in heaven, actual graces, and the Holy Spirit. We just can't go wrong. The forces of evil are great and powerful but the power for good is greater. If we cast our lot with Jesus and all that He offers, we can make it despite the fact that we live in the den of iniquity.

NOISE: You might wonder how noise can possibly interfere in the flow of generosity on the part of the Holy Spirit. It is not only possible but it is a reality. The human person is not made of steel. Human attributes are very sensitive and delicate. Noise impedes transmissions from the head to the heart, from the heart to the head, from God to the person, and from the person to God. If you are traveling on the highway listening to a particular station on the radio, when you get to a certain distance away from the source of transmission, you will encounter static. Noise is the static in the transmissions within the human system between God and man and between man and God.

How many times have I personally come upon a situation when I call someone on the phone. They answer, and then interrupt, "Excuse me, Father, I have to lower the volume on the TV. I can't hear you." And how many times have I been talking on the phone with a mother, who in the middle of one of my sentences, shouts to the kids in the room, "QUIET, I'm on the phone." Noise is either external or internal. These are examples of external noise. Internal noise is the restlessness that a soul encounters by being unsettled and out of peace. It is also the lack of power over the fleeting thoughts of the mind and the multiple cravings of the heart.

To enjoy a clear communication from the Holy Spirit, as He speaks to your mind and heart, your soul must be at peace. It is an absolute must that you pull away from others to assure yourself the silence that Scripture speaks of: "Be still, and know that I am God. " (Ps. 4:10) and: " Be still before the LORD and wait patiently for him."(Ps. 37:7) The heart must come to the assistance of the head here. It is the heart that must internally sound off a definite and serious, "BE STILL! " to all of segments of its internal kingdom. When this is done, the Holy Spirit will come through loud and clear. When speaking with Him your inner voice need be but a whisper. Within the confines of the heart, sound-proofed by its own regal order, the secrets of two hearts are shared.

BUSINESS: "But, Father, I am so busy. How can I possibly spend an hour with the Lord?" Isn't this a fact. We are busy people. It was thought that when the refrigerator, the vacuum cleaner, the clothes and dish washers came into our homes, that we would have a lot of time to pray and to do other things. It did not turn out that way. Partly because the television was thrown in to boot. "If you want something done, give it to the busy person," as the saying goes. To be busy is part of our culture. It is not saying that what we are busy about is always for our best or the best of others. But, it is a fact of life that unless we are stricken by sloth or severe illness, we are on the go. Many, many make demands on us, and we ourselves are one of the many. Jesus gives this lesson, "Martha, Martha, you are anxious and worried about many things. There is need of only one thing. Mary has chosen the better part and it will not be taken from her." (Luke 10:41-42) Mary her sister was sitting at Jesus' feet giving heed to His Words.

The answer to this blockage is to prioritize. First things first! What is recommended here is for you to set aside time for the Holy Spirit. St. Francis of Assisi said to one of the friars, "If you are too busy to pray, then you are too busy." Select a certain time for prayer. Some people find that the best time is early in the morning before everyone else gets up. Others find the best time to pray is late at night, after everything is done and it is quiet in the house. This is one of the things that many people procrastinate about. There must be a strict firmness with one's self to set a time for quiet spiritual reading and reflection. It is as necessary as showering or having lunch. You might want to ask the Holy Spirit to help you learn from Him when would be the best time for your prayer and reflection.

You may find an additional blockage or two in your own life-style. The above are the ones that occur most often. Do not allow yourself to become discouraged. You could read through them, and exclaim, "Oh my, I have ALL of them. What hope is there for me?" Take counsel with the Holy Spirit. The first thing that He Himself would want for you is to help you to clean up your spiritual cholesterol. It is also a priority for Him. No one knows better than He how necessary it is for you to have a blockage-free channel between Him and yourself. Freedom from all blockages may be called "The Holy Spirit Connection." It is yours to have. Work on it but be patient with yourself.

CHAPTER 28

Your Heart and Pain, Pain, Pain

> "Then He said to all: 'If anyone
> wishes to come after Me, he must
> deny himself and take up his cross
> daily and follow Me.'"
>
> *(Luke 9:23)*

> "Whoever does not carry his own
> cross and come after Me cannot be
> My disciple."
>
> *(Luke 14:27)*

*P*ain is something that every person in the world experiences. No one is an exception. In fact, it could be stated categorically that from the beginning of mankind, there has not been a single person who has not suffered pain. Pain is part and parcel of the human experience. If we believe that whatever God creates is good then pain must be good. If we believe that God is a loving Father then pain must be coming from Him as He either permits it or sends it our way because He cares for us and knows that ultimately it will do us some good. To say that God is punishing the world is true, but to say that He punishes the world because everyone is evil, is not true. Mary, the Mother of God, had pain; perhaps more than anyone except Jesus. She is sinless and, yet, she suffered.

We are aware through the Word of God in Scriptures given to us by the inspiration of the Holy Spirit, that before the Fall of our first parents there was no pain. Pain entered into the world after that Fall. So, it can be concluded that pain and Original Sin are connected. Pain is the result of the disorientation that entered into Adam and Eve after they took their eyes away from God and put them onto themselves. Pain is the result of their sin of disobedience. Disobedience is disorientation because God put human beings into the world in the first place to enhance His glory and to share His happiness with them. Adam and Eve were given a free will so that, instead of being made to obey God as all of the other creatures on earth were doing, they were to choose to obey. They were to obey by choice rather than by necessity. Because they chose to disobey, God dealt with them in a different way than He did with Lucifer and the angels who followed him. They were banished immediately from their prestigious place before God and were put out of Paradise. God gave Adam and Eve and their posterity a punishment but only for a time. It was in God's plan to send a Redeemer Who would save all human beings from their sins and allow them, finally, to enter into His presence to enjoy the happiness intended for them before the Fall.

The Redeemer did come. He was the Son of God Who took on flesh through the power of the Holy Spirit and Who was conceived in and born of the Virgin Mary. It was in the divine plan that Jesus would suffer, and His suffering would atone for the sins of all mankind. He did suffer excruciating pain; first by humiliations, then by a scourging, wearing a crown of thorns; carrying His own cross to the place of executions and, finally, by being crucified. At His death, after undergoing what He did, the gates of heaven were opened for mankind. All who believe in Jesus as the Redeemer and obey His Words, would enter heaven; immediately, if the debt for their own sins was satisfied, or after a period of purification in Purgatory.

If Jesus died for our sins, why is it that we still have to suffer pain? Redemption has been accomplished. However, before humans can receive its full benefits, they, according to the plan of the Father, are to tap in to the sufferings of Jesus by their own. The consequence of Christ's redemptive action was the atonement to the Father for the sin of Adam and Eve as well as for all the sins of mankind. In order for redemptive action to benefit the individual, each soul must be washed clean by the Sacramental waters of Baptism. This cleans the soul of the stain of Original Sin. It remains now for each person to cooperate in the Father's redemptive plan by accepting his/her sufferings as indebtedness to Him for personal sins committed. One's sufferings are to be joined with the sufferings of Jesus. Adding our personal sufferings to those of Jesus atones to the Father for our personal sins.

In addition to being baptized, each person must work out his salvation. Heaven was never to be a pure gift. It was to be earned. It is an outright gift to children who die in their innocence after baptism. All others, by divine plan, are to earn Heaven. This is done through a free obedience to the teachings of Jesus and by walking in His footsteps. Part of what He did was suffer. If He suffered for me in advance, it is for me to pay Him back by my personal suffering. The human mind cannot possibly fathom all of this. The human mind, illumined

by grace, knows that one's suffering is necessary and beneficial when joined to the suffering of Jesus. As Christians, it is
our belief that our suffering adds to the suffering of Christ and
makes it possible for us to atone for our own sins and for the
sins of others. Our suffering, when joined to the suffering of
Jesus, advances God's plan of the redemption of the human
race. St. Peter in his first letter throws some light on the
subject. "Dear friends, do not be surprised at the painful trial
you are suffering, as though something strange were
happening to you. But rejoice that you participate in the sufferings of Christ, so that you may be overjoyed when his glory is
revealed." (I Peter 4:12-13)

The suffering that we endure is meritorious. It is registered
in heaven and will be a source of reward for us there. The
greater the suffering, the greater the reward. Suffering offered
with great love for sinners is most pleasing to God when this
suffering is connected with the suffering of Jesus. Suffering is
not to be sought as an end in itself. When it is borne with
patience and resignation to the Will of God, it is received by
God and applied where it will do the most good. The best
possible path for our suffering is that it be given to Mary, who,
in turn passes it on to Jesus; He, accepting it from her, offers it
to the Father, who receives it with greater delight than if we
offered it to Him directly. It is because of the dignity of the
person offering it that its value is enhanced because it is
offered to the Father by His Divine Son.

It would also be helpful if we realized that through the
offering of the Sacrifice of the Mass, Christ's redemptive action
continues to produce fruits. The Mass is a continuation of the
Sacrifice of the Cross. It is confected in an unbloody manner
by way of a mystical death. As the priest pronounces the
Words of Consecration, first he says, "This is My Body... . "
Then he continues with, "This is My Blood... ." When, in ordinary life, the blood is separated from the body, death ensues.
This separate consecration is essential for the validity of the

Mass. It is through it, that the Sacrifice is effective. It is essentially connected with the redemptive suffering of Christ.

There are some practical aspects that can be mentioned now to help you take up your daily cross and accept the sufferings that come your way. First, make a general intention each morning to offer your sufferings to Jesus to be applied wherever needed within the family of the human race. Second, know that your suffering can be recycled. For example, they can be directed for the benefit of the poor souls in Purgatory. That, of course, can be part of your general intention. Third, take on voluntary suffering such as Mother Mary encourages you to do by fasting and doing little penances.

Here are a few suggestions to help you humanly handle pain when at times it seems unbearable. The mind does not help. The more it concentrates on the pain, the greater the suffering. The more it hurts, the harder it is to offer it personally to Jesus because of the fact that it is being resisted. For you to learn to say "yes"to the pain as you are suffering it, is putting your heart into it and making of it a loving gift.

To stay with the pain itself rather than distancing yourself from it by simply holding on to the thought of it brings an additional cohesiveness to your physical and spiritual system. When you invite division within yourself in your pain, it intensifies and tends to become unbearable. If you find that you cannot handle it, do not feel guilty if you take some pain killer. It was God who had the greater part in the invention of Aspirin. The mind continues to add to your pain by reminding you that you have suffered this pain for two years and that you will probably have it for the rest of your life. That is unfair. Sufficient for the day is the evil thereof. Another principle is: divide and conquer. To take each day as it comes and with the power of the will, to cut off the memory of yesterday and prevent the mind from passing on to think of tomorrow and days beyond is something positive. It might be a relief to your sensitivities to know that because animals do not reflect on their pain, they suffer less than we think. It is the same with children. Their little systems react to the pain right to their screams and tears but, because their minds are still inactive, they do not reflect on their pain therefore it is more bearable than we adults would think. They need compassion, and all that goes with it, but it is a blessing to them that they have not yet grown up. In your own pain, put your mind on the pain of Jesus on the cross and it will be easier for you to bear up under your own pain.

You might glance again at the Scripture readings at the beginning of this chapter. If the Lord recommends that you pick up your cross daily, that means He intends for you to set it down. You cannot pick it up daily unless there is an opportunity for you to free yourself of it on one occasion each day. Now, when might that be? I would suggest that it be when you go to bed. Once you climb into bed, slide the cross under the bed. It will be there for you to pick up in the morning. That is not as ridiculous as it may seem. If You allow yourself to have a good night's sleep and you become well rested, you will have new energy in the morning. You will be able to handle the pain much better for the whole day. Now the trick is to have a good night's rest. It is your undisciplined mind that is usually the cause of restlessness, nightmares, and worries. When your mind continues to be active all night long it causes parts of you to not rest. That is why at times you are more tired in the morning than you were when you went to bed. If you would but turn off your mind, you would have a much better rest. You would enter a state of complete oblivion. You would sleep so well that you would not even know that you are sleeping. One of the secrets is to fall asleep lovingly. If your night's occupation is in the heart instead of the head you will sleep well. It would be the same if you fell asleep obeyingly. "Jesus wants me to sleep, OK, I will." When you are obeying, you are in your heart and the heart has a greater absorptive power than the head.

How considerate of God to have created different flavors of pain. Just think if we all had the same pains, we would get no sympathy. Then too, if we compare our pain with that of Jesus, we can handle it better. Also remember that God is most helpful when we are in pain. Prayer is good medicine. The Holy Spirit dwelling within you is well aware of your pain. He is the One Who can help you to cope with it and to receive encouragement to recycle it.

A great quandary would arise within you were you to ask yourself the question, "Should I bear this pain, or should I ask Jesus to heal me?" That does offer a problem to many. To put the matter into the care of the Holy Spirit is the shortest and quickest solution. Being able to follow His prompts and His nudges will bring relief in the face of doubt. He will remind you that no pain is being offered to you greater than, with the help of God's graces, you can bear. God does not give us a heavier cross than He knows would be counter-productive. You do not ever suffer alone. Your Guardian Angel, Mary, your Mother and Jesus are right with you. The greatest assistance comes when you are given the power to be resigned to your pain, and to be able to say with Jesus, "Father, not My will but Your Will be done." There is no benefit for you to compare the size of your cross with anyone else. It's a trap! Once you put your mind onto your suffering, you bungle it. Keep your heart in the foreground and allow it, with the help of the Holy Spirit, to cope with your cross rather than try to question why God gave it to you or why He gave you such a heavy one. Learn to accept it and go on with your life. Remember the secret word, "recycle." It will give you a lot of mileage. Remember, too, that the natural heart has absorptive power. This plus divine assistance makes even the greatest pain bearable.

CHAPTER 29

How to Pray with Your Heart

"Then you will call upon Me and come and pray to Me, and I will hear you."

(Jer 29:12)

"When he arrived at the place he said to them, 'Pray that you may not undergo the test.' After withdrawing about a stone's throw from them and kneeling he prayed, saying, 'Father, if you are willing, take this cup away from Me; not my will but yours be done.'"

(Luke 22:40-42)

Our Blessed Mother, over and over again, pleads with Her children to pray with the heart. For years she has been asking for this. At times she does come forward and acknowledges Her disappointment with us and, at times, even unto tears. Why does she have to ask so often? It is because we don't listen. Why don't we listen? We don't listen for one or both of two reasons, or both. The first is that we don't know how to pray with the heart. The second is that it's too demanding. It takes more effort than we are ready, or able to give. Why don't we know how? It is because no one teaches us. Why do we have to be taught? It is because it is not easy to find one's heart. Why is it so difficult to find the heart? It is because we look for it in the head. Good answer! When we know how, why is it that we don't make the effort to do it? It is because the effort won't come. Why doesn't it come? It is because our wills are too weak. Why is it that some find it too demanding? Because there's too much that has to be done in order to get ready for it. No more questions. You get an A+ for your answers.

Prayer has caused a lot of problems for a lot of people. Basically because there is a lack of understanding of what it is all about. Even the apostles asked Jesus to teach them how to pray and they were right there with Him. Let's go through a few basic truths concerning prayer.

First of all, there is a difference between saying our prayers and praying. To say prayers or to read them from a prayer book is fine. It is the easiest but not the best, way. If a person cannot pray then saying or reading prayers is better than nothing, especially if one says them or reads them using one's heart. Do you remember when Jesus asked His apostles, "Who do people say that I am?" They gave various answers. Then He asked, "And Who do YOU say that I am?" I make this observation. You and I know that it is much better to say a few words from one's own heart than to read someone else's words. The Lord could say to the one reading, "Very well, but now, what do YOU want to say to Me?"

The Sacrifice of the Mass is a prayer of the highest caliber. It is a liturgical function that demands participation. It is not a matter of watching or even of listening. Each person is to be alive and give it his or her best. That means that the heart participate. When it comes time for the response, "Lord, have mercy," There are different levels of responding. It could be made automatically from the top of one's head without even thinking about the words. The response could be made with thought on the words but no heart behind them. The response could be made with thought, and only one-third heart; with thought and only two-thirds heart. What is expected, however, is that the participation be made with full attention, and with the WHOLE heart. "That's tough!" I know. It becomes easier when one prepares before Mass begins by becoming quiet inside and outside, in the same way that we would prepare to meet with Pope John Paul II person to person. And yet, Jesus is JESUS! He's REAL, and He's RIGHT THERE!

It's enough to make one cry to see what is going on in the church before Mass starts. The enemy has done this to us. There is a simple weapon that he used, so simple that no one needs to think twice to discover it. It came right from Satan. Here is what he introduced, not directly, of course but by some of his helpers. Listen, how simple. "We are all brothers and sisters. We are a community. We are a family." GREAT, BUT we are a family with GOD as our FATHER. We are in HIS HOME! The weapon used was, "Let's introduce and put emphasis on the HORIZONTAL put aside the VERTICAL. We have used the vertical too long. People need a CHANGE." That's it! It is a simple "slight of hand" trick. If you look at a cross you will see the vertical bar and the horizontal bar. Notice that the horizontal bar would not stay up by itself if it were not attached to the vertical bar. The vertical bar has to be first then the horizontal bar can be affixed to it. What the enemy did was to slip away the vertical bar and chose simply to promote the horizontal bar. In some places the vertical bar is laid aside or out of immediate sight.

The vertical represents my personal contact with Jesus. It is to be a loving and living friendship. He talks to me and I talk to Him. We converse with each other. After we converse and express our warmth to each other, then, it is Jesus Who sends us to our brother and sister to share with each the love that we personally have with Him. Now, if everyone first goes to Jesus and becomes very warm and loving, then each can share HIS love with the other. The parish community is not a FRATER-NITY. It is BROTHERS AND SISTERS of the Loving FATHER. It is HE Who must receive recognition FIRST, and not only recognition, but also RESPECT and REVERENCE. We should make it a point to visit with our brothers and sisters in the vestibule, parish hall or outside. There are a number of parishes that have socials after the Sunday Masses somewhere within the parish precincts. That is laudable. The church where Mass is celebrated is a church, that is, a building consecrated to GOD, not to the community.

Once we get things in order and recognize what it is that we are in church for, then it is altogether a different experience. We are to breathe, sing, respond, listen, receive Holy Communion with REVERENCE. To ignore or bypass the Vertical — Jesus, is the work of His archenemy.

Prayer is either ORAL or SILENT. Oral prayer is not just saying words but saying words that come from the heart. It is a joint action of the head and the heart. The words are spoken or read with the warmth of love. This is the way that all prayer should be. This includes our participation at Mass giving the responses. It includes the recitation of the rosary, all of our private prayers, our novenas and chaplets. It is saying special words to God with a warm heart; that is, meaningful words spoken to God or one of His Saints with LOVE. All vocal or oral prayers should be contained within a balanced diet. Just as when we eat we look to have a balanced diet of proteins, carbohydrates so it must be with our prayers. The balanced diet of prayer can be abbreviated into the word, "A-C-T-S." "A" is for Adoration, "C" is for Contrition, "T" is for Thanksgiving, and "S" is for Supplication. If we find that we are always asking God for favors, and ignoring the other three, we don't have to wonder why many of our prayers are not answered. We are USING God for our own benefit. We are praying very selfishly.

The second part of that division of prayer is, SILENT prayer. It is called silent prayer because there are no words spoken either externally nor internally. Silent prayer is again divided into MEDITATION and CONTEMPLATION.

Meditation is entered into when one reads a part of the Scriptures or some holy book, stops reading, and meditates on what was read. In community meditation, someone reads while the rest of the community listens. When the reading is over everyone goes into their heart and head to give serious thought to the contents of what was read. After a time (fifteen or twenty minutes) there is more reading (about five minutes) and again everyone enters his/her soul and reflects. When the meditating is completed, a short conclusion is read to assist those who participated to remember the main point around which the meditation took place.

The second form of silent prayer, contemplation, is a bit different. There may be some reading but not nearly as much as in meditation. Once the participants enter into prayer, each depends on the Holy Spirit to activate the mind and the heart. It is the Holy Spirit Who takes the initiative. The soul takes an active/passive part that is, the soul acts in giving itself to the Spirit, and then it allows itself to be impressed upon by the Spirit. Impressed means that the Holy Spirit illumines the mind and inspires the heart for the purpose of being able to converse person to person using no words. The Holy Spirit takes the initiative to draw us close to Himself, to the Father, to Jesus and, at times to His Beloved Spouse, Mary. From this form of prayer there is a close union of mind and heart with the "Mind and Heart" of God.

Our Lady would be pleased if we prayed with the heart with words spoken with love. To enter this latter form of prayer with the heart is contemplation. Our Lady would be ecstatic. Even

our Holy Father has asked all laity to enter into this form of
prayer, because our evil times demand that we get deep, deep
into prayer. When there are trees on the top of a high mountain which has strong winds, the trees are prepared to put their
5   roots deep into the soil so as not to be toppled over. Because
of the strong winds of immorality, Our Lady and the Holy
Father are pleading that we go deep into prayer so that we
would not be "toppled" over into compromise with the evil.
Yes, this form of prayer takes a lot of work but only at the
10 beginning. It can become part of one's spiritual lifestyle. It is
easier to get into than one might think because the Holy Spirit
gives assistance either to the mind or to the heart or to both. In
this form of prayer, the head takes the back seat as the head.
The heart makes use of its own mind. Recall when the shep-
15 herds visited the stable and reported to Mary about how they
came to know of the birth, it was said of Her "Mary treasured
up all these things and pondered them in her HEART." (Luke
2:19) In your reading of the previous chapters, especially the
one on the dignity of the human person, I would ask you to
20 remember Who it is that would be engaged with you in your
contemplative prayer. It is the PERSON of God. What dignity is
yours to be able to enter into a love relationship with your
GOD. Here you are, but one of the trillions of human beings
that God created, and YOU are able to have a private time with
25 Him, Person to person. No wonder that this prayer requires
preparation! Your first step in this preparation is to remember
that you are a lowly creature with dignity and that God is your
Maker, your Redeemer, your Sanctifier.

The second step in preparation is for you to come to the
30 state of BEING. Being? Yes, being. You are a human BEING, are
you not? Come to the state of "who" you are. God did not
make you a human "doinger." Doing was not experienced by
you when God first created you. Being was the first thing. You
just "Be'd" in your mother's womb. So to come to the state of
35 being is to do what? Just to BE! Allow your life to come out of
you equally, with no concentration of life coming more out of

one part of you than any other. Allow yourself just to go
"PLOP." Your mind must stop thinking, your heart must stop
wishing, your body must come to "no motion." (You might
keep on reading, if you like, and then later return to reread all
of this for the sake of putting it into practice, step-by-step.)   5
Why do you have to come to being? Because that is what God
is, He is the Supreme Being. Whatever He does, He does with
His whole BEING. So, this is where you are to meet Him, in His
Being, not in words or feelings or in any active human experience. You are to meet Him in TRUTH. You are primarily a   10
human BEING. Being is the common denominator between
you and God.

Here is the third step. You are not just a BEING, You are a
DEPENDENT Being. You are dependent on God for every
single breath, for every single heartbeat. Without God, you   15
would not live. Your dependent being comes in contact with
the Supreme Being. Your head may not go out ahead of you.
Your whole being is to go out to God's whole Being.

No need to strain your brain to try to figure it out. Take it
simply as it is: You are a dependent being. Accept the fact of it.   20
There is more to life than doing, there is being. Jesus said
many times, "BE believing, BE trusting, BE loving, BE obedient,
BE forgiving, BE grateful." In our culture, we find this a bit odd.
People around us in other cultures find us odd for all we do is
do, do, do,do and do. "Doing" is not the better part of us. By   25
nature, we are human beings. No need to work on all of this
right now. You can do that later.

In prayer with the heart, the body must play its own part. As
human beings, we are composed of body and soul. Each has
a respective responsibility in this form of prayer. If the body is   30
rigid, so is the soul. If the soul is rigid, so is the body. If you
enter prayer with anxiety or stress, your body will be stiff. Such
an approach will get you nowhere. What to do with a rigid
body? Thaw it out. Give it orders to soften up. First, find somewhat of a comfortable position; not too comfortable, though or   35
you will fall asleep. Then, one by one, starting with your

ankles, your thighs, your tummy, your shoulders, and your head, loosen up so that there is no stiffness in any of these parts. This will require practice. As a result of practice, you approach prayer with your body and soul at peace. No
5 thought. No wish. As a totally dependent being which is reflected in body and soul, you are almost ready to have the Holy Spirit to take the initiative in your prayer.

The fourth step is your breathing. BREATHING? Breathing. In our fast-living culture, we have slipped into the habit of
10 breathing like puppy dogs in short, fast surface breaths. Our blood needs oxygen for its health. If we breathe without any depth, it gets very little. Nor do we want to take in too much oxygen so as to cause the brain to hyperventilate. This is extreme and could be harmful. If you could be awake while
15 you are sleeping, you would know how breathing is at its best. You can tell when a person is sleeping by the long deep breaths he or she takes. That is the normal way of breathing. In our culture we like shortcuts. This is one that we should pass up. Proper breathing of good fresh air is important for the
20 health of body and soul.

If you want to stop now and give it all a brief try, OK but be patient because, at the start, it is not that easy. The great draw-back in beginning is the fact that there tends to be the temp-tation to watch yourself to see if you are doing it correctly. It is
25 understandable at first but that part must come to an end as soon as possible. If you are watching yourself, you are thinking. In this form of prayer, the mind must become still and go into a receptive mode or a listening stance to be able to be enlightened by the Holy Spirit. If you are thinking, He will not
30 force His way into your mind. Your mind must be still and in the state of reception. If you check on yourself to see if you are in that state, your mind becomes active and the Holy Spirit will have to wait till you are ready.

The fifth step is to activate your image-maker. Some people
35 call it the imagination.

I find it better to stay away from that word because it has lost its true meaning. God gave each one of us an internal camera. With it, we can bring images into our mind at will. If you have a daughter at college in a distant state, you could sit yourself down and have a picture of her in your mind's eye and, with your heart send her some love. In most people, especially those who watch television by the hour, this faculty has grown stiff. If you did not use your right arm for a week, it too would grow stiff. I would advise you to enliven your image-maker by practicing to bring before your mind's eye the faces of people you know, places you have been at, activities you had entered into in the past. To do this, it is necessary for you to be in a most relaxed state of body, mind, and will. There is no need to do this now. You can come back to it.

Being in the heart and making use of the image-maker is an exciting combination. A wife who is miles away from her husband can allow her image-maker to bring forth a mental picture of her husband and, with her heart, she can express love for him. Strange as it may seem, her love for him could go deeper this way than if he were standing right next to her. When she is loving him in this manner, she is loving him in a spiritual way with her soul. The soul knows a deeper love than does the body. Of course, this also works from him to her. He can be at work, take five, and allow love for her to rise within his spirit. If both would take time to practice this, they could be united in spirit even if they are miles apart. This is also true between parents and their children. They can be miles away and still be loved by them. Children, when they are older and live in a different city, can do the same.

In short, there are only three things necessary: first, to be in a state of quiet; secondly, to be in the heart; and thirdly, to activate the image-maker. Getting into the habit of living and loving in this manner would put extra excitement into the life of the family.

Now, for the finale. Under the influence of the Holy Spirit one can make use of this manner of loving with the soul to enhance one's contemplative prayer. All it takes is to allow your image-maker, prompted by the Holy Spirit, to present you with a picture of Jesus, a picture of the Father, a picture of Mary, a picture of the various saints, and, even a picture of a loved one who has gone to heaven. The same requirements as mentioned above are, of course, necessary. One must come to the state of dependent being, enter into an inner quiet, place the image-maker into the care of the Holy Spirit, and allow Him to inflame your heart with love. The great difference between doing something with family and friends is that the Holy Spirit takes the initiative in making the connection between your soul and the heavenly Beings. I bring up your loved ones because if they lived a life of goodness, you can trust that even if they are still waiting to get to heaven, they can be prayed to privately.

The above manner of praying opens up a brand-new vista. As much as you know the life of Jesus by heart, you can allow the Spirit to bring up within your soul, making use of your heart and your image-maker, a living experience of all that the gospels reveal to us of the life of Jesus and Mary. The rosary could serve as a basis for both meditative and contemplative prayer as well. The difference is that in the latter, you allow the Holy Spirit to bring before your heart and mind the various episodes of the life of Jesus as found in the Gospel. The Gospel can come alive to you and you can become a part of it by allowing the Holy Spirit to put you right in the middle of any scene reported therein.

With the help of the Holy Spirit, you could go back in time and allow your soul to be with the Holy Family in Bethlehem, with Mary at the Presentation. You can experience the fear of the Apostles as they are in the boat during the storm with Jesus fast asleep. You can be right there when the woman taken in adultery is spared her life by Jesus. You can be there at the trial of Jesus, as He carries His Cross, as He is crucified. You can experience deep in your heart the Resurrection, the Ascension, the coming of the Spirit upon the people assembled in the upper room. In contemplative prayer the Gospel comes to life. You become a part of all that it contains.

You may think that the above is far beyond anything that you can ever get into. Don't underestimate the Power and Love of the Holy Spirit living within you. He is real. He is there. Why not make use of Him to make your prayer life come alive? It is yours for the asking provided you prepare yourself in the way discussed above. A proper prayerful disposition is essential. It is helpful to know that the Holy Spirit will even help you to become disposed to this form of prayer. He will make contemplative prayer easy for you when you give Him the opportunity to do so.

Granted, contemplative prayer does not come easy. But with good will and effort on your part it is yours to have. It calls for patience in waiting. You are to wait on the Lord. If you watch yourself waiting, you are already sabotaging the preparation. Go plop. Loosen up again and again until it becomes second nature. You may not realize what our modern way of life has done to you with the fast pace, worry, anxiety, pressure, stress, many things having to be done, more than what is comfortable. All of these have put a great dent into the human nature that God gave us. The people in Jesus' time were much more at ease than we are. It's probably why He came then, rather than now.

You have now the skeleton. All you need is to be filled by the Holy Spirit. You have heard the expression, to be "filled with the Holy Spirit?" You have put yourself in readiness for Him. You have given Him space within which to work with you You have made yourself available to Him, disposed to receive His Light and Love. The difficult part is not to watch yourself. When you began to drive a car, you were very cautious and you kept your mind on what you were doing. After a time, it all became second nature. So will it be in this beautiful and fruitful form of prayer. Much patience will be needed. Patience and trust. When you have done all to prepare yourself, then the rest is up to the Holy Spirit. Trust is your best inner quality to have while being patient. When you trust, you draw the Holy Spirit as a magnet draws a piece of steel. If you watch yourself to see if you are trusting, then it all stops. Remember, practice makes perfect.

5   There is one thing more that I want to assure you of as you enter into the posture of contemplation. You will become more receptive to graces. If you give up your rigidity, your soul will become ready so that on a day-to-day basis, the Holy Spirit will be able to share His Life with you. He will pass on to you

10   some of His energy. He will bring warmth and gentleness to your heart. He will give to you a greater agility of body. You will be less tired. You will need less sleep. Every part of your life will improve. You will become a better mother, a better father, a better organizer, and better in so many other things. It will all

15   come in faster the more trust your soul enjoys. In order to make this happen more quickly, begin to ask the Spirit to help you with your lack of trust. When gradually you allow Him also to work on your spiritual cholesterol, you will indeed have a change of life. Peace and joy will be found more often within

20   your soul. You will increase in faith, in love, in humility, in virtue at large. I repeat, right now, TRUST is the most important spiritual experience. Pray for it. Work with it. Allow it to become an integral part of your personality.

CHAPTER 30

Your Heart and the Fullness of Life

*"I came so that they might have life
and have it more abundantly."*
(John 10:10)

*"For to the man who pleases Him,
God gives wisdom, and knowledge
and joy."*
(Eccl. 2:26)

*A*ll this and heaven too! This is what Adam and Eve enjoyed when they basked in the riches of nature in the Garden of Paradise. To pass with the mind, enlightened by grace, from the present moment back to that period of time, one must pass through centuries of events that have a bearing on our spiritual life today. To read through the history of the Old Testament and to be saddened over the failure of our first parents hits the heart deeply to know that the span between their life and the joys of heaven has been lengthened by centuries of painful expectation. The understanding that there were those human beings who would never make heaven simply because they failed to learn by the mistake of the first man and woman on earth is to add salt to the wounds. Looking at this scene through human eyes, with a heart softened by grace, what must it have done to the Creator to see that these two people messed up His plan to have all those He created with Him in heaven.

Because He was God and loves His creatures, He promised a Savior Who would make all things right so that heaven could still be the permanent home of all humans. To read the history of the New Testament, especially the part that has to do with the life and teachings of the Savior, becomes a breakthrough from the darkness of the skies of the sufferings of the early people to the joy that their difficult journey did finally lead them to heaven. The loss of heaven for some must still have left some regrets in the Divine Heart. Death, the price to be paid to the Father, by the Son made Man finally fulfilled the dreams and hopes of many as it opened the gates of heaven for them.

The history between the opening of those gates and the present time is long and tiresome to read. It seems that from generation to generation, despite the Savior's greatest efforts through His Church, through the Holy Spirit, and through His Mother, there were good times and there were evil times. There were the times when humans followed the way of the Savior and there were also times when many followed the example of Adam and Eve, despite the accomplishments of the Redeemer. Though the gates of heaven were opened, many people did not seem to care whether they were or not.. Some did, and having believed in Jesus and returned to the inner state of their souls known by our first parents before their failure, did enter heaven. For this present generation, the dreams of many are still enveloped in the hope for heaven's endless joys. There exists, however, the greatest clash of all times between that part of humankind which is following in the footsteps of the first offenders who are walking toward heaven by taking the road pointed out by the Savior. For those of the first part, who pay no heed to the heaven promised by God, have succeeded in making their own heaven right here on earth. The smaller part still pines for the fulfillment of the promises made by the Savior; that the real heaven is not too far off and will be reached by the short way of the Cross. In the meantime, the battle between the two parts continues and it seems that it is getting more fierce than ever.

The Father, humanly speaking, must be saddened over those of His children who wish not to be with Him in the heaven that He made for them but choose their own eternity with the same demon who stole the dreams of heaven from our first parents. The pain of anticipation for the time when everything will be peaceful and the Father puts the whole world in order is at times most difficult to bear. It is all taking so much time and the waiting for it to be settled is hard to take. The promise is what makes the pain of waiting tolerable. "Pick up your cross daily," paraphrasing Jesus, "and if you continue to carry it you will be found worthy to enter into My Kingdom."

Jesus promises you and me the fullness of life. Is this to be here on earth, or must we wait for heaven? Let us recall the catechism lesson that teaches that, if we are living in the state of Sanctifying Grace, we are already beginning to live in heaven at least we are on the right road that leads there. As we continue step-by-step to carry our cross on our shoulder, in imitation of Jesus, the cross becomes lighter and the heart feels happier with each step. Could it be that our entrance into heaven is to be a gradual one rather than all of a sudden? It would seem so, for by beginning to experience the fullness of life that Jesus promised here on earth we are already in the "vestibule" of heaven as we enjoy experiencing a life of grace.

The challenge of today is to find the road that leads to the fullness of life on this earth which was given to us by Jesus and following it step-by-step each day, until we find ourselves within the grand domain of heaven itself.

It all began when God envisioned each one of us and brought us into existence. He blessed us in a unique way by arranging for our Baptism. It was our first meeting with the Holy Spirit. We grew a bit and then received Jesus in our first Holy Communion. Everyone told us that Jesus loved us and that we were to love Him back. So we did. Confirmation was our next step in the journey through which we got just a little better inkling of the Holy Spirit. We were told that we now were soldiers of Christ and so were ready to defend Him against His enemies. It was then that everything went into oblivion. We went through years of growing up, getting through years of schooling, making friends, having fun and a few tears. Going to Confession once a month and attending Mass every Sunday were things we were expected to do. Life, with all that it offered, was confusing. It offered things to be happy about and things to be sad about. We were expected to avoid sin, and to remain in the state of grace. We were reminded that Jesus was the real Jesus in the Eucharist Whom we should periodically visit. Each one of us entered into our particular vocation in life and made efforts to do things right.

To find the road to heaven for yourself is the beginning of your true spiritual life. For you to have been placed on it, can be a help, and it can be a hindrance. It can be a help if everything in the Faith had been explained to you, as much as explanation can be given. Part of the explanation is to learn that it will not be possible to understand everything in the Faith. There are truths hidden from the mind for which you must take God's word. Being put on the road can be a hindrance if it was done without sufficient explanation. When young people find themselves on the road and begin to question others about it, if they do not receive satisfying explanations, they leave it; some for a time, others for good. There are people who are led to the road by the Holy Spirit. They not only stay on it and follow it religiously with its bumps, ruts and potholes, but gain so much that they invite others to join them and are knowledgeable enough to lead and instruct them.

When you entered school, you did not learn everything right away. Then, you were on the road to gain knowledge. It is the same on the road to heaven. You won't learn everything right away. It will take you years. In fact, it will take continuous learning for a lifetime. There will always be something new to know. Reading good solid spiritual material and listening to others who are qualified to teach will be of great help to you. The Church, as the Mystical Body of Christ, is Christ in our midst. Through it you can receive all sorts of information and help along the way to make it easier for you to travel.

By what has just been said, you can see why it is important for you to choose to be on the road. It's important for you to say, "I WANT to go to heaven when I die," or, 'I WANT to obey God," or, "I WANT to save my soul," or, "I WANT to learn more about my Faith." Any one of these "want to's" can get you started on your own, even if you had been simply put on the road by means of being born into the Faith and received Baptism, Confirmation. In that case, it would be a good idea for you to explore what the Baptism you received was all about. You might choose to reexamine Confirmation, wondering what it was that happened to you when you received it. Learning about all of the basics of the Catholic Church is necessary even if you were exposed to the life within the Church in your early years.

The road to heaven has a number of paths that lead to it. There are various points of a reentry after having received Baptism, First Communion, and Confirmation. It could be a path that brought you onto the road through the death of someone very dear to you. It may be the tributary of being invited to take part in a prayer group. It may be that you married a spouse who is a good practicing Catholic or, on the other hand, a non-Catholic and you want to be able to give reasons for your beliefs. There are almost as many paths to the road to heaven as there are people who choose to take it.

Sooner or later, you will find that on the road to heaven there are times when you allow yourself to grasp, examine, or rethink something through. There is time when you are to use your will as in the case of believing and loving. There are times that you use body and soul together as you would when you genuflect. There are times when you turn your mind in reverse and do some listening instead. There are times when you speak to God out loud as during the Mass when you respond to prayers. There are times when you love Him without words as when you spend time with Him after Communion. There are times when you sit and do nothing. You allow yourself just to BE with God as two people who love each other; they don't speak, but they just want to BE with each other.

The longer that you stay on the road the more you learn. In your traveling, little by little, you are putting your life in order. This is one of the most exciting things that happens. Life by its complications tends to bog you down. Confusion, because of complexities, leads you either into detours or dead ends. As a result of Original Sin, disorder entered into the world and into human beings. Emotions and passion erupt, and sometimes explode. Feelings want to run the mind. The mind is derailed from pure reasoning by strong wishes. The heart is hardened because of unexpected hurts from people. Many things crop up unexpectedly in life that could overpower you or even lead you into sin. It becomes a full-time task just to keep your life in order. You will find along the way antidotes, solutions, spiritual medicine, counseling service, and encouragement. You will find that you can stop sit yourself down, and have a heart-to-heart talk with God. You can find some joy to help you in your sadness. You can find people traveling along with you who are able to give you answers to the questions you never knew you had. You'll experience a personal closeness to Jesus, a strengthening of your soul by the Holy Spirit. There is no end to how many things in your life you could put into order while you travel day-by-day.

There is a marvelous guarantee that everyone who travels the road in time will gain what Jesus came to give to each traveler. That is, fullness of life. That could mean many things to many people. To Jesus, it meant only one thing. He let it be known that if and when you follow His Way of Life, you would find the total fulfillment of your being. You would receive a happiness that would fill your soul like nothing else could in the world. In truth, this is what the human heart craves for and lives for. It will be yours when your life is perfectly ordered; when every part of you is doing exactly what it was meant to do by God's design. It will be tantamount to the happiness that Adam and Eve had before the Fall. That happiness is not the same happiness that will be yours in heaven. There, you will have the Beatific Vision, that is, you will see God as He is, face-to-face. Here the happiness will be so complete that it will be enjoyed in the midst of sorrow, while still bearing the cross. It is happiness that the world cannot give, for it does not have it to give. It is the happiness that every human being craves but, sad to say, only a few will live to merit it.

The world looks for quick fixes. It takes the barrage approach with the hope that something will work. Everything is tried and everything ultimately turns sour. The human heart recognizes the real thing because the attraction for the real thing was planted within it at the time of its creation. It is looking for the infinite response of love, and when it does not find it, it keeps on looking. Jesus, with His offer of the fullness of life, not only plotted the course to achieve it but He guaranteed every single individual all the assistance necessary finally to enjoy it. If the world would only turn to Jesus. The WORLD? If millions of His so-called FOLLOWERS would only do that.

How many billions of humans will never make it. This is what caused Jesus the greater part of His agony in the Garden of Gethsemane. He knew that His suffering and death would be to no avail to the greater part of humankind. The major cause for the failure of the greater part of humankind is its obsession with the body. The greater part of the world's people do not have the slightest inkling of what the soul is. Most of the people on earth live only a surface type of human life. They concern themselves with thoughts and emotions. For them there is nothing beyond that. Their thoughts beget feelings, and the feelings of most people govern their behavior. They either feel like doing something or they do not feel like doing something. It's one or the other. There is no depth of life. Why? Because they have not come across a particular sentence in Sacred Scripture in which Jesus says, "I am the Way, the Truth, the Life." (John 14:6) They do not recognize the Messiah or, if they do, they make little or no effort to respond to His call.

This may come to you as no surprise. It happened at the very time when Jesus walked the streets of this world. It happened when the leaders of the Chosen People who were the Scriptures scholars of their time, failed to recognize the Messiah when He came. There are some leaders in our own Church today, Christ's One, Holy, Universal, Apostolic, Church, comparable to the Pharisees who fail to recognize the signs of the times. Could it possibly be the same kind of blindness that plagued the Pharisees?

Everyone enjoys shortcuts. The greatest shortcut to the fullness of life is to fall in love with Jesus Who is the Way, the Truth, the Life. Jesus has not simply established a religion with do's and don'ts. He has established a way of life. His Church is not an organization. It is an organism. It is living, vibrant, and ready to deliver that fullness of life offered by its Founder, namely, to love Jesus and to allow oneself to be loved by Him. That's the ultimate. That and that alone completely satisfies the human heart and makes all of its cravings to disappear.

The showdown between the forces of good and the forces of evil is upon us. It is the battle between Christ and the Antichrist. It is war to the finish between Michael and the fallen Lucifer and their respective angels. It is the conflict of all conflicts at which time Jesus will establish His reign and evil will be banished from the earth. It will be a time when heaven will come close to earth and only those who have fallen in love with Jesus and remained faithful to Him will come through victoriously. It may seem like an oversimplification to say this, but truly it is precisely this, that has and continues to be cause of the rift between the good and the evil. It is the battle between the HEAD AND THE HEART! Which one is to be given preeminence? Satan said to Adam and Eve, it's the head. Jesus, the Messiah, the One Who makes all things right, continues to promote the heart. It is not either/or, it is a matter of which one takes dominance over the other. Is it the head over the heart, or the heart over the head? Jesus says it's the heart over the head. The heart will give the head its proper due. The head will not give the same to the heart.

When the heart is held in the spiritual life, as it is held in the physical life, it is able to give life to the soul just, as in the phys-ical realm, the human heart gives life to the body. The spiritual heart will elevate the mind to a dignity that is fitting for what God made it to be, the receiver and the transmitter of truth. When the heart is given its own dignity, it is able to lift the mind to its proper lofty place by making it possible to generate believing thoughts, trusting thoughts, loving thoughts, obedient thoughts, forgiving thoughts, grateful thoughts, reverential thoughts, adoring thoughts, coping thoughts, disciplined thoughts, that is truthful thoughts.

The fullness of life, the heights of happiness that will satisfy the human heart cannot be obtained unless and until a person is able to find his/her way to a life of the heart. It is not I who am saying this, it is Jesus Who said it a long time ago and it is He Who is still saying it through the Magisterium of His Church. Consider too the two great Commandments.

In our day, consider the presentations of the Sacred Heart of Jesus and the Immaculate Heart of Mary. The message of the preeminence of the heart is obviously being promoted by Them and all of heaven. What is the world lacking most in all of its boastful accomplishments? They have all been brought into being through pride, brought on in our day and by the so-called brilliance of the human mind. The question is asked once again. What is the world lacking most? It is love and love comes from the heart. It is unending and satisfying happiness and this comes only from the heart; a heart loving its Infinite God and Infinite love being given in return.

In the Gospel of St. John, the fifth verse of the fifteenth chapter says of the Lord, Jesus, "I am the Vine, you are the branches. If a man remains in Me, and I, in him, he will bear much fruit; apart from Me, you can do nothing." God IS Love. Jesus IS God. In order to enjoy the fullness of life, you and I must allow His love to pass through our spiritual veins. Everything we do, if it will have any value before the Throne of God, must come from and through Jesus. Whatever good you and I do must be because Jesus wants us to do it. He wants us to bring every action of our everyday life under the common denominator of "Jesus wants me to." Every action of that sort will register in heaven. Every such action, selfless and under the Will of God, will reap dividends that are out of this world.

In the final analysis of what life is all about and what is to be accomplished here on earth, Jesus once again makes it unmistakably clear. It is as follows:

"For I was hungry and you gave me something to eat, I was thirsty and you gave me something to drink, I was a stranger and you invited me in, I needed clothes and you clothed me, I was sick and you looked after me, I was in prison and you came to visit me.'"Then the righteous will answer him, 'Lord, when did we see you hungry and feed you, or thirsty and give you something to drink? When did we see you a stranger and invite you in, or needing clothes and clothe you? When did we see you sick or in prison and go to visit you?' "The King will reply, 'I tell you the truth, whatever you did for one of the least of these brothers of mine, you did for me." (Matt. 25:35-42)

It is the expression of compassion extended to one's neighbor in need, done as the branches of the Vine, that is the ultimate form of behavior in life and the one which merits the fullness of life.

If the world at large turns its back on Jesus, it also turns its back on the Holy Spirit. If there is a lack of sanctity and love in the world it is because the Sanctifier and Love Personified is not welcome within its precincts. This is not only true of the worldly of the world; it is also true of those within the Fold who externally are within the Sheepfold but are only disguised as sheep. The Holy Spirit is the Giver of Life. He has the responsibility to keep the Barque of Peter afloat. His Power is the Power of Love and not of force. Those of us on the sidelines may wonder why the Holy Spirit does not purify the Church. It is because the plan of the Father is to let the weeds grow with the wheat till the end. Then they will be separated.

CHAPTER 31

In Conclusion, and Beyond

"Well done, my good and faithful servant. Since you were faithful in small matters, I will give you great responsibilities. Come, share your master's joy."

(Matt. 25:21)

*P*erseverance is an experience of the will. If you have faithfully continued the journey from the beginning until now, you are in your heart. Praise God for that! The journey has offered you a challenge for life. This is the state of being for every Christian, but especially for one who in true sincerity wishes to and chooses to draw closer to Jesus to the degree of being able to experience the beating of His Heart. This means: that you accept His Love for you and return it more and more so that gradually you can say to Him, "Jesus, I love you with my whole heart" and hear within your own heart, "And I love you with my whole Being and have done so from all eternity."

Your journey from the head and the heart has ended and yet it begins again. It is easier the second time around. I suggested at the start for you to make use of these chapters as you would an owner's manual. Refer to them when you hit a situation in real life. When you do, hopefully one or the other practical directives will come in handy.

Time is short! Of this I am certain. Make hay while the sun shines. While there is still a flood of mercy coming forth from the Blessed Trinity, take advantage of it. Allow yourself to live under the influence of the Holy Spirit. Become aware of His prompts, which will be directed to your heart and soul for the accomplishment of some action, and of His nudges which require no thought or willful action but require a docility of spirit. He nudges you into an action without consulting with you or giving you reasons for the nudge. You will find yourself in a place without knowing how you got there or why you are there. It was His power that put you there. and it is He Who knows why you are there. In time, you will find out.

A living, personal relationship with the Person of the Holy Spirit will serve you the best and assist you more quickly and more genuinely to achieve the fullness of life. The most important experience to bring to yourself and His greatest input into your life, is that of trust. Trust Him implicitly. No questions asked. Just do as you are prompted to do and go with docility to where you are nudged to go. At times He will send you to Jesus. At times He will bring you to Mary. Remember as The Holy Spirit and Mary brought Jesus into the world for the first time, They are now preparing to bring Him in for His glorious return. It is also Their responsibility to take care of you and to transform you to make of you another "Jesus." Jesus will bring you to the Father. The Father will send you back to Jesus, Jesus to Mary, and Mary to the Spirit. Because you have made the effort to do more than was comfortable, they see in you a likely subject for Their special love.

One of the ways that you will win an immediate response from the Holy Spirit is for you to tell Him from your heart, "Holy Spirit, you may love me." He waits for your invitation to act more fruitfully within you. Such expressions as, "You may heal me," or, "You may teach me," or "You may be generous to me," will turn out to be very beneficial. But remember, NEVER watch Him. It is a breach of your trust to do that.

In closing, I would like to give you a simple list of things to remember and to dip your spirit into. Even if you work on one or another of them once a month, you will find that you are making progress in your spiritual life and that the fullness of life will be yours in the measure of your generosity to the Members of the Trinity and to your Mother Mary. May you receive an unexpected surprise of a particular blessing for your efforts to grow.

If ever you would be moved to gain a very personal and intimate relationship with the Holy Spirit, I would recommend reading the book entitled, "The Sanctifier" written by the late Most Reverend Luis M. Martinez, the onetime Archbishop of Mexico City. It can be ordered from the Hearts to heart Center, P.O. Box 212, Rensselaer, N.Y. The cost is $8.95, plus $3.00 priority mail. It is not the easiest reading but even if it takes you a year, it would be well worth your while. It must not be read with curiosity. It must be read with a sincere heart, with faith and trust. Next to the Holy Scriptures, I would advise a serious reading of this book to help you to tie together all of the segments of your spiritual life.

I take the liberty of imparting my priestly blessing upon you and send it to you by way of "angel express." May God truly bless you for the effort you made to travel this journey and the sacrifice of perseverance that had to accompany your effort.

Following is a list of one-liners for you to munch on whenever you are prompted to do so by the Holy Spirit:

1. Know when you are in your head, and when you are in your heart.
2. You are not your mind, you HAVE a mind.
3. The pitcher never pitches until the catcher is ready to catch.
4. You cannot think and listen at the same time.
5. "Jesus wants me to ...".
6. The Holy Spirit is your Divine Guest.
7. The Holy Spirit never tires of hearing that He is welcome.
8. "I was hungry and you gave me something to eat."
9. "Jesus, You may love me."
10. "Jesus, You may bless me."
11. I WANT to be good!
12. I WANT to be holy!
13. At the name of Jesus, every knee will bend.
14. I can recycle my pain.
15. Be not afraid!
16. Divide and conquer.
17. What's next, Lord?
18. Good morning, Your Highness!
19. One Hail Mary from the heart is better than fifty-three from the head.
20. Take one day at a time.
21. At night, slip your cross under the bed.
22. I am not a "WHAT," I am a "WHO."

23. I don't "gotta" do anything until I WANT to.
24. Satan can get into your head, but not into your heart.
25. Too much thinking gives the Holy Spirit a busy signal.
26. Keep your nose to your own grindstone.
27. Put blinders over your eyes.
28. Breathe like you breathe when you are sleeping.
29. "Can you not spend one hour with Me?"
30. Learn from Me, I am meek and gentle of heart.
31. "Unless you change and become as a child …"
32. If your body is rigid, so is your soul.
33. "Come aside and rest awhile."
34. "Come to Me all you who labor, and I will give you rest."
35. "If today you hear His Voice, harden not your heart."
36. How are you doing with your spiritual cholesterol?
37. Make hay while the sun shines; it's mercy time.
38. The church is God's House.
39. Pray with your heart.
40. There is more to life than doing; there's BEING.
41. Don't put off till tomorrow what you can do today.
42. Think twice before you speak.
43. Selfishness is one thing, self-love is another.
44. One hour spent with Jesus is better than a thousand years without Him.
45. If you cannot find something good to say about someone, say nothing.